IMAGES
of Rail

FLORIDA RAILROADS
in the 1920s

D1497597

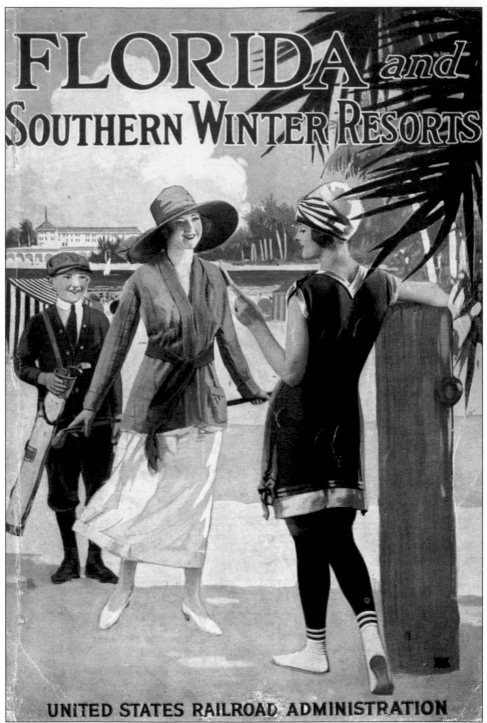

FLORIDA and
SOUTHERN WINTER RESORTS

UNITED STATES RAILROAD ADMINISTRATION

America's railroads were controlled by the federal government during the First World War, including those in Florida. In an effort to bolster tourism, the U.S. Railroad Administration occasionally released booklets like the one above. In March 1920, the various companies were returned to their rightful owners—the stockholders.

IMAGES
of Rail

FLORIDA RAILROADS
in the 1920S

Gregg Turner

ARCADIA
PUBLISHING

Published by Arcadia Publishing
Charleston, South Carolina

Printed in the United States of America

Library of Congress Catalog Card Number: 2005934872

For all general information contact Arcadia Publishing at:
Telephone 843-853-2070
Fax 843-853-0044
E-mail sales@arcadiapublishing.com
For customer service and orders:
Toll-Free 1-888-313-2665

Visit us on the Internet at www.arcadiapublishing.com

For Professor Dr. Jeffrey S. Turner, a world-class educator,
distinguished academic author, and a great brother.

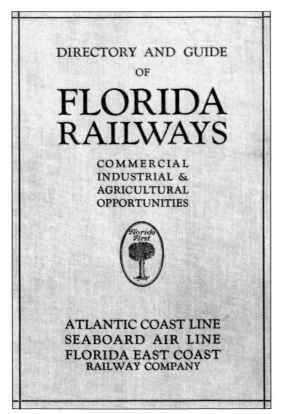

This directory was issued in the 1920s by Florida's three biggest railroad companies. Together the "Big Three" operated over 85 percent of all railway mileage in the state. What they achieved that decade is the subject of this book.

CONTENTS

ACKNOWLEDGMENTS

Several individuals and organizations helped shape this work. With much gratitude I acknowledge Prof. Seth Bramson, distinguished corporate historian of the Florida East Coast Railway; Larry Goolsby, Seaboard Air Line and Atlantic Coast Line Railroads Historical Society (aclsal.org); Dawn Hugh, Historical Museum of Southern Florida (historical-museum. org); Jim Shelton, history department coordinator, Tampa-Hillsborough County Library; Laura Katz Smith, Dodd Research Center, University of Connecticut; as well as staffers at the Railway and Locomotive Historical Society (rlhs.org), the National Railway Historical Society (nrhs.com), and the Florida State Photo Archives.

Special thanks are also owed to Sam Boldrick, Don Hensley Jr., Jeanne Hickam, Mike Mulligan, Ken Murdock, Russell Tedder, and Ted Shrady.

Regretfully it is not possible in this brief work to cite every fact or event that occurred on Florida's railroads during the 1920s.

Readers with comments or questions are welcome to contact me at the e-mail address below.

—Gregg M. Turner
GreggTurner@msn.com

Florida's Sunshine

FLORIDA with its tropical sunshine, its endless mileage of bathing beaches on the Ocean and on the Gulf—the gentle breezes crossing innumerable Central Florida lakes laden with the aroma of the orange blossom—yachting and motor boating in waters mirroring the colors of the tropics—polo—golf—tennis—racing at Hialeah, Pompano and other courses—all amid scenes of unsurpassed and beautiful surroundings, is without equal in this or any country. The proximity of Florida to Eastern and Western points is emphasized by the one-night-out-on-time service offered by the Seaboard Railway System over its own rails without change or interchange south of Richmond.

S. DAVIES WARFIELD,
President.

January 8, 1927.

The Seaboard Air Line Railway greatly expanded in Florida during the 1920s land boom. Its president, a Baltimore banker, was deeply enamored of the state, as this little ad helps confirm. But as we will see, the Seaboard's expansionary measures came at great cost.

INTRODUCTION

Florida's railroad heritage began in the 1830s amidst Native American upheaval and territorial colonization. Eventually the "Iron Horse" conquered the state's vast interior; linked every population center; brought in the tourists; and ably conveyed the wealth of Florida's mines, forests, factories, groves, and farms. Today, nearly 175 years later, railroads still remain a dependable source of transportation within the Sunshine State, even if their golden age has come and gone.

Thus far, Florida railroad history has embraced two extraordinary periods of development: that which manifested in the 1880s and the epic chapter that unfolded in the 1920s. When the first era began, about 500 miles of railroads existed in Florida, a somewhat diminutive figure in light of the Sunshine State being larger than England and Wales combined. However, when that decade closed, nearly 2,500 miles could be counted—a 480 percent increase. The surge was attributable to many factors, including the resumption of state land grants, the ready availability of capital, and the work of several spectacular developers like Henry Plant, Henry Flagler, Henry Sanford, and William Chipley.

Eclipsing this era were the prolific events and milestones of the 1920s. Virtually every initiative of that fabulous period was undertaken by Florida's three biggest companies—the Florida East Coast, the Seaboard Air Line, and the Atlantic Coast Line Railroads. Never before had the "Big Three" invested so much capital in Florida, by one estimate well in excess of $100 million. New lines and shortcuts resulted, hundreds of miles of double track were installed, heavier steel rail was laid, countless bridges were strengthened or replaced, new cars and locomotives appeared, automatic signal systems were activated, yard and terminal facilities were built or enlarged, new trains were inaugurated, and dozens of new stations arose. Further the frequency of railway service within and to the state reached an unprecedented level. When the 1920s ended, the railway map of Florida stood at its greatest extent—some 6,500 miles (double tracks, yards, branches, and sidings included) compared to the 2,800 or so that are in service today.

The primary reason why the Big Three undertook these expansionary and improvement measures was simple: Florida was experiencing a colossal land boom, one of the greatest migration and building episodes in American history. During the 1920s, people flocked to the Sunshine State as never before, where real estate transactions and get-rich-quick schemes abounded. Countless new homes were built that decade along with hotels, apartments, and commercial buildings. Even new cities surfaced, such as Hollywood-by-the-Sea, Boca Raton, Coral Gables, and Venice. All this generated an enormous railroad passenger and freight business.

Before the boom, railway traffic on the Big Three moved in a predictable fashion. Citrus and vegetables went north between October and May. Heavy southbound passenger traffic began in late fall and reached its peak in the latter part of February, only to shift north until late April. The remainder of the year was marked by light business of all kinds, with train service reduced to a minimum.

According to the November 26, 1927, issue of *Railway Age* magazine, the first traffic abnormalities were detected in March 1920 when "many new people came to Florida, a growing interest in real estate surfaced, and numerous construction projects were started in Miami, West Palm Beach and points north along the east coast." By 1925, the usual May lull never occurred, as people from every section of the country poured into Florida as never before. Orders placed by Florida merchants, the up-tick of passengers, coupled with one of the largest citrus and vegetable crops ever, placed an enormous burden upon the "Big Three" that became increasingly difficult to carry. There was also wild speculation in all classes of commodities, for brokers and dealers ordered supplies far in excess of actual requirements. Often shipments were sent to Florida with no definitive destination, changing hands many times en route and arriving at destinations where inadequate or no service tracks existed. Before long, thousands of freight cars became stranded in the state and choked the movement of traffic. The scenario was also complicated by the arrival of thousands of empty refrigerated cars, which were used to move perishables to northern markets.

This unprecedented congestion produced a gridlock, which prompted a hurried meeting of traffic officials. An embargo was subsequently called that took effect October 1925. Except for foodstuffs, fuel, perishables, and a few essential commodities, no other freight traffic was permitted to enter or move within the state. When the embargo was called, about 4,000 freight cars were jammed in the Jacksonville yards. Another 8,000 were held at outlying points such as Atlanta; Cincinnati; Washington, D.C.; St. Louis; and New Orleans. Gradually order was restored, and the embargo was completely lifted in May 1926. By then, though, the boom had fizzled.

Two ferocious hurricanes pounded Florida in the fall of 1926. Further the critical supply of real estate buyers vanished, a string of bank failures began, the Mediterranean fruit fly attacked the state's citrus crop in 1927, and the stock market crashed in 1929. This fantastic canvas provides the backdrop for our story, how the Big Three responded to these extraordinary times.

One

THE FLAGLER SYSTEM RESPONDS

No transportation entity was better positioned to reap boom traffic than the Florida East Coast Railway (FEC). Its single track mainline descended the peninsula's eastern coastline and penetrated every setting of what the railway liberally hailed as "The American Riviera." At the boom's height, one dozen passenger trains dashed back and forth between Jacksonville and the "Magic City" of Miami. Some even went beyond to the island city of Key West, where awaiting boats took excited passengers to continental Havana. If one impediment plagued the FEC when the boom began, it was lack of capacity, an issue that was eventually erased at great cost.

FEC president William Beardsley, a one-time financial confidant to FEC founder Henry Flagler, orchestrated the railway's initial response to the boom. However, the real task of increasing capacity and modernization fell to William Kenan Jr., who became president in 1923. His sister, Mary Lily Kenan, became Henry Flagler's third wife.

The FEC was released from federal wartime control in March 1920. At that moment, the company operated 764 miles of track, notably a main line between Jacksonville and Key West together with eight branches, the one leading down to Okeechobee being the longest. Most of the company's stock was held by Flagler's trust fund. (Among its trustees were Beardsley and Kenan.) Revenues that year amounted to $13.7 million, while net income totaled $1.3 million.

Free of government control, Beardsley resumed the task of installing heavier steel rail on the company's main line. Further, several new stations were built, new houses for track workers were erected, and improvements were made to the yards at South Jacksonville, New Smyrna, Fort Pierce, Buena Vista, and Key West. Additionally, all major wooden bridges on the main route were reinforced with steel beams, many passing tracks were constructed, and a number of new engines and cars were purchased.

The railway's financial results hardly changed in 1921, though postwar improvements accelerated. Fresh ballast was applied to the main line, a new general office building was begun at St. Augustine, and 175 boxcars were equipped with ventilators to help move perishables to northern market. In the following year, some $600,000 was spent on new locomotives and rolling stock. Beardsley controlled operating expenses in 1922, which helped produce a $3.2 million profit.

William Kenan Jr. assumed the reins in 1923. When Flagler died in 1913, Mary Lily Kenan Flagler stood to inherit her husband's $100-million estate, provided she outlived the trust fund.

But Mary died in 1917, and her estate, which included the Flagler fortune in trust, now passed to William Kenan and his two other sisters. Thus, the Kenan family had both a fiduciary and proprietary interest in the Flagler System of rails, hotels, land companies, and boat lines. Kenan's power solidified in 1925, when the former industrialist became board chairman.

During 1923, the FEC purchased additional steam locomotives as well as rolling stock. Kenan's board also approved construction of a new, double-track drawbridge over the St. Johns River at Jacksonville. Also the existing drawbridges at Stuart and Jupiter were rebuilt while important additions were made to the New Smyrna shops. Government approval was also received that year to extend the company's Okeechobee Branch down to Lemon City (near Miami) together with a branch near Lemon City to Larkin (South Miami).

Kenan reached a critical crossroads in 1924. Either he had to dramatically increase the railway's capacity in light of boom traffic, or he must sell the property to a larger player. The Atlantic Coast Line Railroad, which the FEC connected with at Jacksonville, made overtures about a purchase, but Kenan chose to keep the Flagler System intact and to modernize the railway. To do this, he restructured the company's finances and issued new bonds along with equipment trust certificates. Proceeds helped pay for one particularly large and expensive endeavor: double-tracking the company's main line between Jacksonville and Miami. Kenan also had the Okeechobee Branch advanced to Pahokee, whose rich muck lands would eventually generate a considerable vegetable and sugar cane traffic. Also the Miami Belt Line was constructed from Lemon City to Hialeah, where a new racetrack had opened. Finally Bowden Yard (Jacksonville) was enlarged, new passenger stations opened at Daytona and Hollywood, and the FEC ordered more locomotives and cars.

Results for 1925 were indeed gratifying. Revenues soared to $29.1 million; net income rose to $3.8 million. Many capacity and improvement projects were completed, including the Moultrie Cutoff (it eliminated the long main line swing through East Palatka) and the massive new drawbridge opened over the St. Johns River in Jacksonville. The installation of automatic block signals was begun that year between Jacksonville and Miami, the Okeechobee Branch was now extended to Canal Point, the Miami Belt Line opened from Hialeah to Larkin, and the yards at Hialeah and Bowden were enlarged. Work also commenced on the sprawling Miller Shops near St. Augustine and a third addition to the General Office Building. Some $4.3 million alone was spent on new locomotives, coaches, and freight cars.

Despite the boom sputtering, Kenan continued to upgrade the FEC during 1926. That year, the main line double tracking project was completed as was the automatic block signal system. Expansion projects at the principal rail yards continued, and the busy Okeechobee Branch was advanced toward Belle Glade. The huge Miller Shops opened in 1926, and the General Office Building was completed. Purchase orders were again issued for more locomotives and cars, outlays that totaled $3.6 million.

Revenues fell to $13.4 million in 1929, largely because boom traffic had dried up. What did not vanish was the company's debt load. Paying interest on all those bonds and certificates became difficult, especially when losses began to accrue in 1927. By 1931, the FEC was in receivership. But woe unto those who thought the Flagler System would implode. It certainly did not.

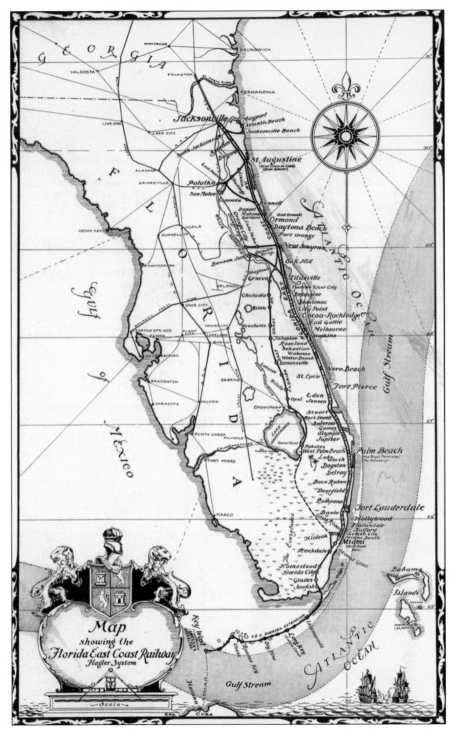

Based in St. Augustine, the Florida East Coast Railway was the only Big Three member whose tracks were entirely contained in the Sunshine State. The territory the company served was stricken with boom fever. In fact, passenger and freight traffic became so intense that the FEC had to install a second mainline track between Jacksonville and Miami.

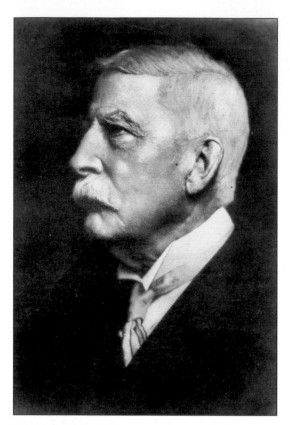

Henry Morrison Flagler (1830–1913) founded the Florida East Coast Railway. The former Standard Oil figure assembled his railroad fiefdom by acquiring existing lines and building new ones. The Flagler System also included hotels, land companies, boat lines, and other business entities.

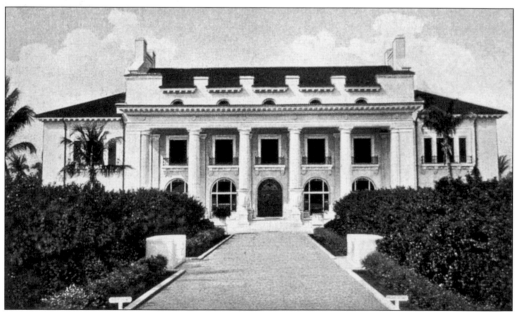

Flagler built a palatial marble estate in Palm Beach (called Whitehall) for his third wife—the former Mary Lily Kenan. Magnificently restored today, the Flagler Museum draws crowds from the world over.

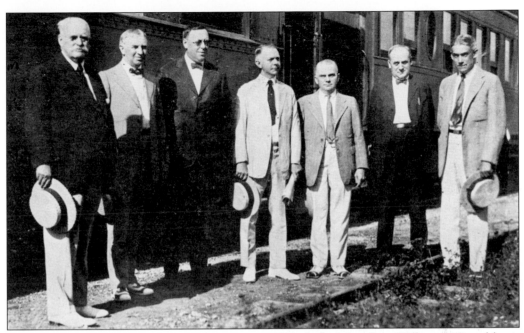

Officials of the Florida East Coast Railway pose in 1921. At far left is Pres. William C. Beardsley, a longtime Flagler confidant and former company treasurer. Next to him stands William Kenan Jr., who succeeded to that position a few years later. (Courtesy Railway and Locomotive Historical Society.)

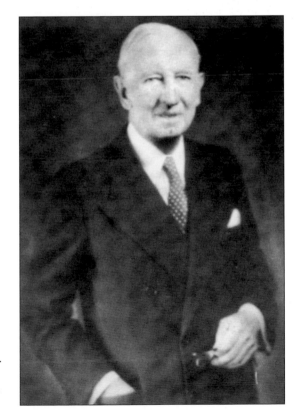

William Rand Kenan Jr. (1872–1965) codiscovered calcium carbide and was active in the acetylene industry. His business acumen attracted Henry Flagler, who involved him with the Flagler System. Kenan's sister, Mary Lily Kenan, became Flagler's third wife. (Courtesy Railway and Locomotive Historical Society.)

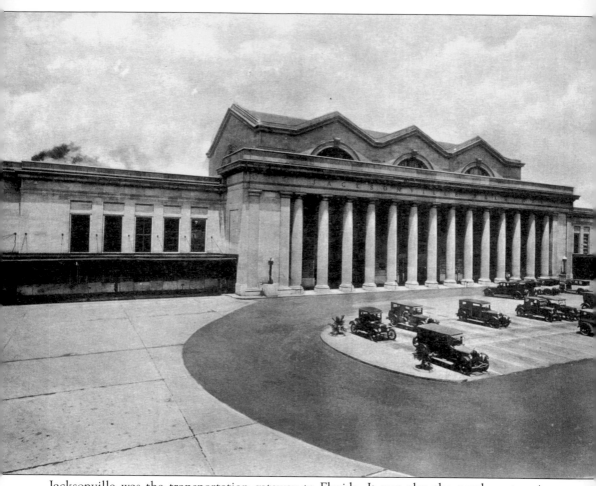

Jacksonville was the transportation gateway to Florida. It was also the northern terminus of the Florida East Coast Railway. Its splendid Union Terminal, which opened in 1919, was owned by several companies including the FEC. Architect Kenneth Murchison conceived the terminal building in the Beaux Arts style. Fourteen colossal columns graced the colonnade. At the boom's height, hundreds of passenger trains came and went in a single day. The magisterial edifice closed in 1974, was later renovated, and today houses the Prime Osborn Convention Center.

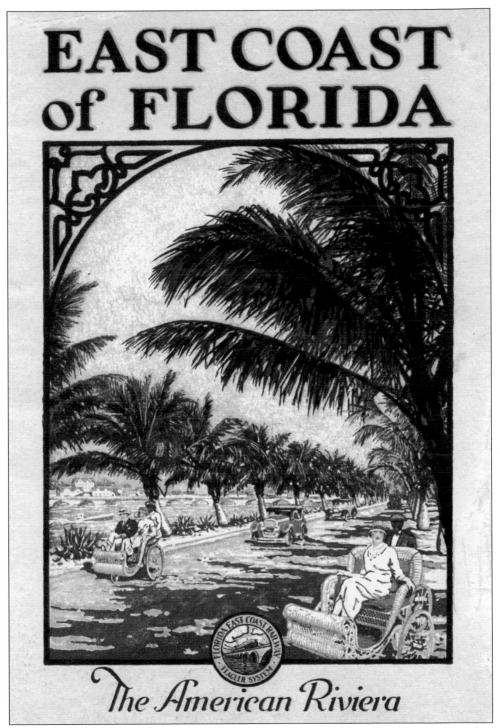

EAST COAST of FLORIDA

The American Riviera

Throughout the 1920s, the Florida East Coast Railway issued beautiful booklets and brochures. The covers were often printed with pastel colors and featured scenes of carefree, pampered living. The company liberally advertised its territory as "The American Riviera." For many, it was an age of effortless riches.

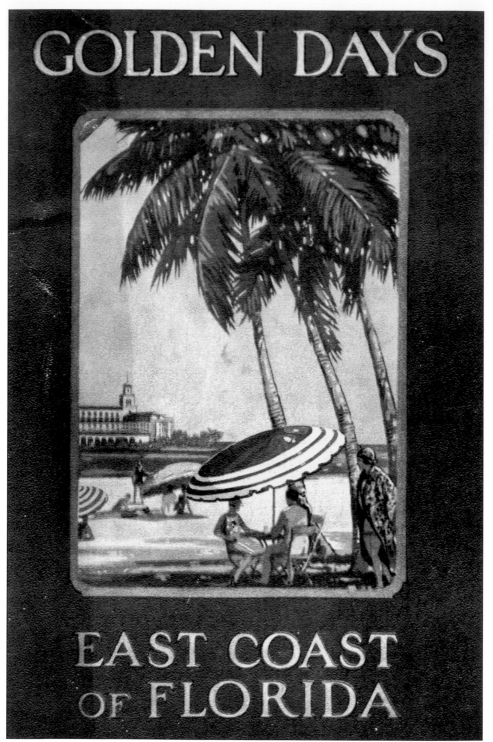

The FEC series *Golden Days* contained information about the attractions and accommodations found on Florida's east coast. Inviting photographs rounded out the publication. After beholding an issue, more than one winter-bound reader jumped on the next train south.

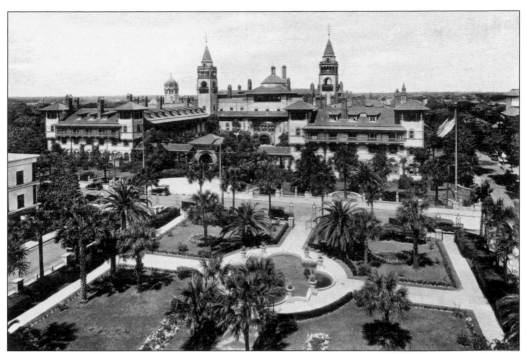

Henry Flagler's first hotel venture was the magnificent Ponce de Leon in St. Augustine. Before long, guests from around the country flocked to the regal setting. Today it is home to Flagler College.

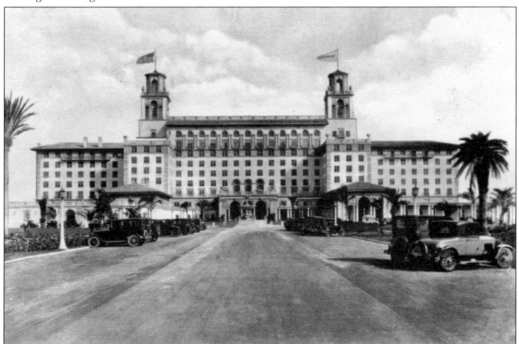

Flagler created Palm Beach, and two Flagler System hotels stood in the posh enclave. Seen here is the Breakers of 1926, which replaced an earlier building. The magisterial setting cost $6 million to build and could accommodate 500 guests.

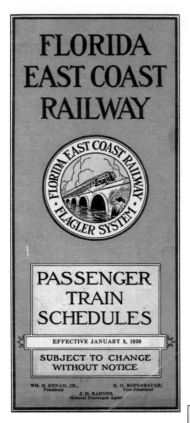

This public timetable was issued by the FEC in 1928. A pen-and-ink sketch of the famed Long Key Viaduct, on the company's Key West Extension, helps form the logo. Today these pieces are prized by railroad collectors, and they fetch more than pocket change.

At the boom's height, one dozen FEC passenger trains dashed between Jacksonville and Miami, including *The Miamian* and the opulent *Florida Special.* Other railroad companies advanced the trains north of Jacksonville to New York.

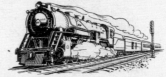

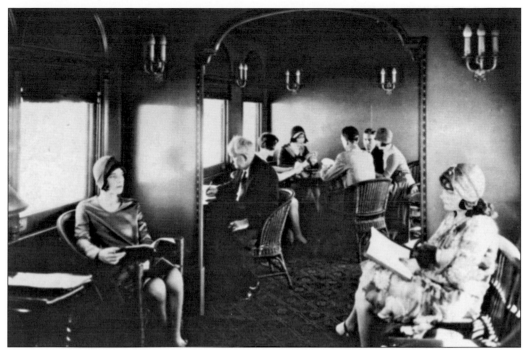

This 1928 image depicts the parlor car interior of the famed *Havana Special*, which ran between New York and Key West via the FEC. Upon arriving at the island city, boats took excited patrons to Havana, which was then nicknamed the "Paris of the Caribbean."

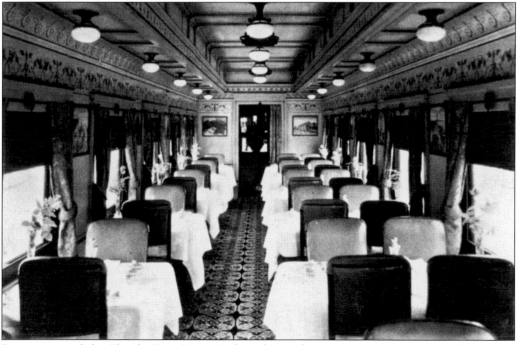

Dining cars of the Florida East Coast Railway boasted an inviting interior. Crisp linen, real silver, and sparkling crystal adorned each table, as well as fresh-cut flowers. Each "restaurant on wheels" was also softly illuminated and richly carpeted.

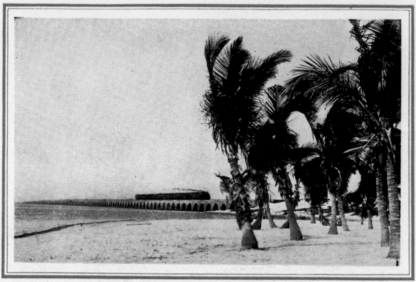

Long Key Viaduct from the island of Long Key.

A Railway Over the Ocean

Although the Magic City seems a fitting climax to our journey down the East Coast of Florida, there still remains before us one of the most beautiful and unusual excursions — a trip over the ocean by rail to Key West.

South of Miami the Florida East Coast Railway passes through Homestead, the commercial center of the Redland District. Then, after leaving Jewfish Creek, at the very tip of the peninsula, the line extends for over one hundred miles out into the ocean over the chain of Florida Keys.

The Over-Sea Extension, as this part of the system is called, is everywhere regarded as one of the most remarkable engineering feats of the age and is often referred to as the "Eighth Wonder of the World." Passing over the series of huge bridges, which were necessary to span the ocean between the islands, land is almost lost to view and the distant Keys appear as faint ribbons of green on the horizon. On either side of the train the clear subtropical waters spread out in an unbroken expanse to the horizon — sublime in coloring, hues as evanescent as those of the rainbow—a sea painted in colors which defy description, merging from jade, amethystine and sapphire into the deep cerulean blue of the horizon. Great fish, swimming lazily in the clear depths, may often be seen from the windows of the train, and, while crossing the shallows, one often catches a fleeting glimpse of the stately pelican, graceful crane and other unusual birds of the tropics.

The Keys themselves, with their palm-fringed beaches, strongly suggest the South Sea Isles. Ninety-one miles south of Miami is Long Key, home of Long Key Fishing Camp, the most famous center in the world for big-game fishing, for the waters in this region literally teem with innumerable varieties of marine life.

The company's Key West Extension hop-scotched over the Florida Keys and open water. It opened in January 1912 and was immediately hailed as "The 8th Wonder of the World." At first, Henry Flagler acted as banker to the project, but when costs proved daunting, the railway issued bonds. As noted FEC historian Seth Bramson states: "The Key West Extension was a railroad construction feat unequalled, unparalleled in U.S. and possibly world history."

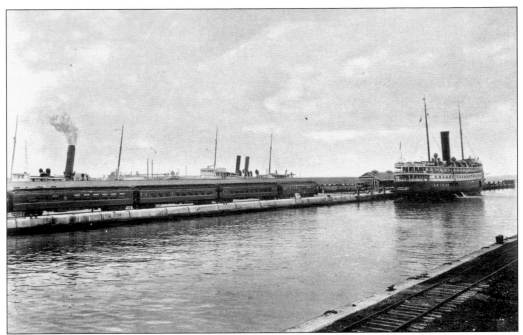

At Key West, the FEC operated a full-service marine terminal. Passengers could board boats for Havana, and a large freight and commodity business was entertained. Curiously this extraordinary extension never generated the revenue streams envisioned by the railway's founder, Henry Flagler.

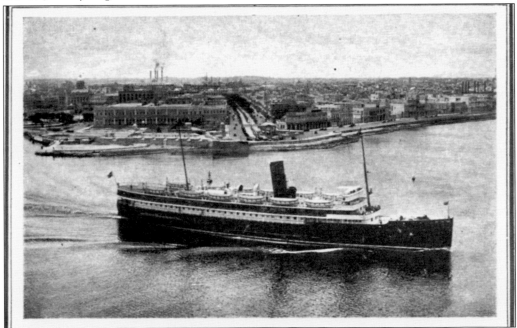

A Flagler System vessel steams into the harbor at Havana. The city attracted the rich and famous as well as the hoi polloi. Its continental atmosphere reminded one of Europe. Hotels abounded in the 1920s as did lovely commercial buildings, stately homes, casinos, and historical settings.

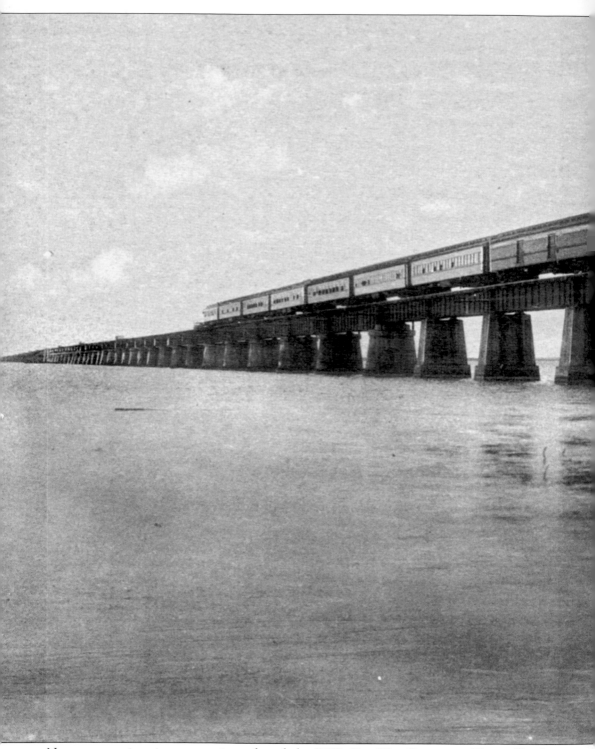

Numerous engineering masterpieces dotted the FEC's Key West Extension. This is Knights Key Bridge, whose steel trusses sat atop concrete foundations. Owing to construction delays elsewhere, the dock at Knights Key became the southern terminus of the extension for several

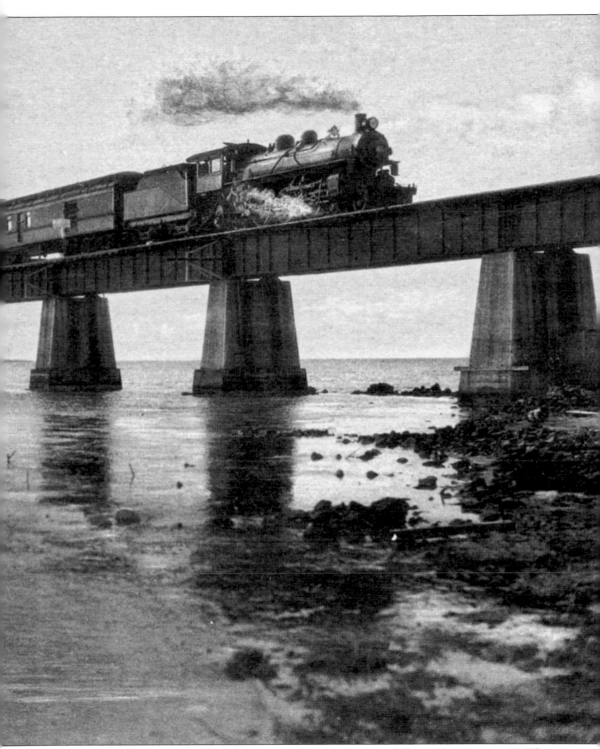

years. Flagler lived to open the fabled project in 1912 but died the following year at age 83. The extension itself was partly destroyed by the horrific 1935 Labor Day hurricane. Later it was converted to a highway.

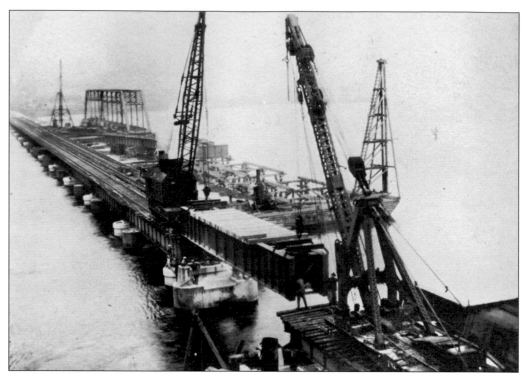

To increase capacity in the 1920s, the FEC constructed a new drawbridge over the St. Johns River in Jacksonville. Spans were literally floated into position, thus railway traffic was minimally disrupted.

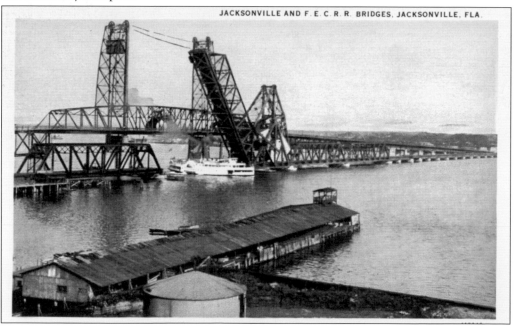

JACKSONVILLE AND F. E. C. R. R. BRIDGES, JACKSONVILLE, FLA.

The new double-track drawbridge at Jacksonville replaced one having a single track. Its bascule counterweights were then the largest ever constructed in America. FEC trains still rumble over the massive structure, which in this 1929 view has opened for a steamboat.

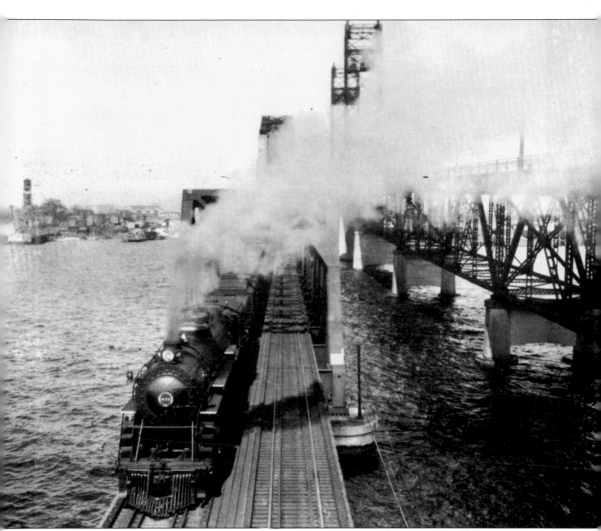

A southbound FEC train is seen here crossing the new St. Johns River drawbridge. The Union Bridge Company of Kansas City fabricated the substructure in 1923. The superstructure was erected by Phoenix Bridge of Pennsylvania. The work was rushed to completion, and the southbound track was opened for traffic in December 1925. A highway bridge is visible at right.

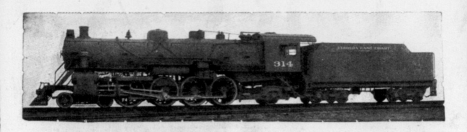

Forgings, Frames and Crossheads Are Vanadium Steel

GREATER strength in forgings and castings, without proportionate increase in locomotive weight, was the aim of the designers of fifteen Mountain type locomotives built for the Florida East Coast.

Carbon-Vanadium, 50% higher in elastic limit, and tougher than plain carbon steel, was specified for:

> Driving and Trailing Axles
> Piston Rods
> Crank Pins
> Main Rods
> Side Rods

Vanadium Cast Steel, which has at least 30% higher elastic limit or useful strength than ordinary cast steel, was specified for

> Main Engine Frames
> Crossheads

For new locomotives and for replacements on existing power, specify Carbon-Vanadium Forgings and Vanadium Steel Frames and other castings. They add greatly to operating dependability, reduce maintenance costs, and eliminate forging and frame failures.

Write for data on Vanadium Steels in modern locomotives.

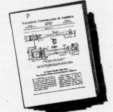

Write for Bulletin LF-1 containing detailed information about Carbon-Vanadium, the tough but simple alloy steel.

VANADIUM CORPORATION OF AMERICA
120 Broadway, New York   Book Building, Detroit

VANADIUM STEELS
for Strength, Toughness and Durability

To modernize its locomotive fleet in the 1920s, the FEC purchased several batches of "Mountain-class" locomotives. They had a 4-8-2 wheel arrangement, burned oil not coal, and could haul both passenger and freight trains. Vanadium Steel furnished many of the locomotive's components.

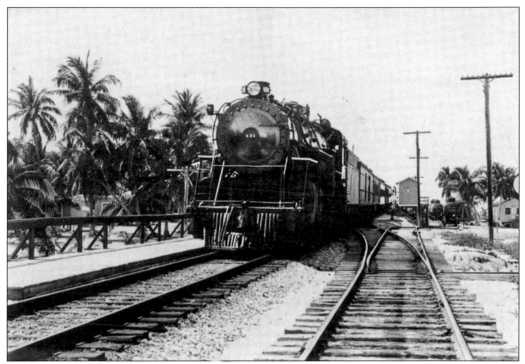

The muscular Mountain-class locomotives even operated on the Key West Extension. In this March 1929 scene, an FEC train briefly halts at Long Key en route to Miami. No. 431 was built by Alco in 1926.

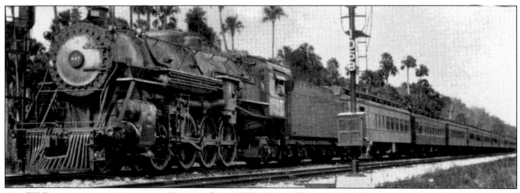

An FEC passenger train nears Ormond in 1928. No. 447, another Mountain-class locomotive, is on the point. Notice the lack of coal smoke, as she and her sisters burned oil.

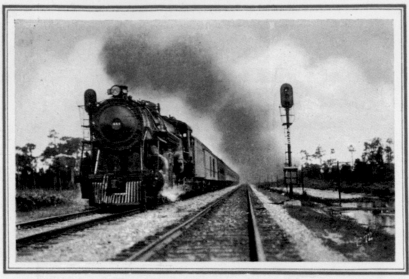

An F. E. C. limited train en route.

This Modern Double-Track System
Reaches All the East Coast Resorts

For the quickest and most enjoyable journey to those golden days along the Gulf Stream, you will travel over the Florida East Coast Railway.

This system, which was the pioneer in the development of the American Riviera, is today the pioneer in improved transportation facilities and service. It is the most modern railway system in Florida.

Following the direct route along the coast between Jacksonville and Miami, the Florida East Coast Railway is completely double-tracked over the entire distance of 366 miles. Every mile of the main line is protected by colored light automatic block signals. Every mile is substantially constructed, laid with heavier rails and thoroughly ballasted with rock. All bridges are double-tracked and of modern concrete and steel construction.

Clean, Cinderless, Dustless Travel Comfort

The Florida East Coast Railway is the only system in the Southeast using oil-burning motive power. For this reason your trip over this route along the interesting American Riviera is exceptionally clean and comfortable — virtually cinderless and sootless. In addition, the heavy ballasting of the tracks prevents dust from sweeping into the cars from the roadbed.

So accurately level and firm is this modern steel highway that your train glides over it with "limousine" smoothness. The finest Pullman equipment designed, including club, lounge and observation cars, provides the utmost travel luxury.

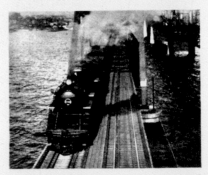

The new double-track bridge across the St. Johns River at Jacksonville.

The booklet *Golden Days* featured interesting articles about the Florida East Coast Railway. This one describes the company's newly constructed double track mainline between Jacksonville and Miami. It was laid with heavy steel rail together with crushed rock ballast, thus passing trains created little if any dust. The installation of automatic block signals was also integrated.

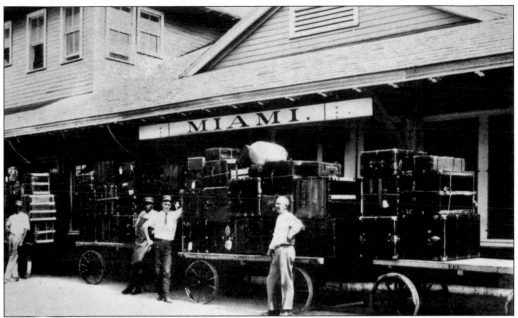

Baggage is stacked high at the FEC's Miami station in 1927. All will be loaded into a train's baggage car. The huge trunks suggest that many passengers packed more than a few days of clothing!

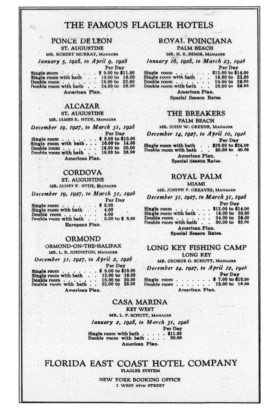

THE FAMOUS FLAGLER HOTELS

PONCE DE LEON
ST. AUGUSTINE
MR. ROBERT MURRAY, Manager
January 5, 1928, to April 9, 1928
Per Day
Single room . . . . $ 9.00 to $11.00
Single room with bath . . . 13.00 to 16.00
Double room . . . . 18.00 to 22.00
Double room with bath . . . 24.00 to 28.00
American Plan.

ROYAL POINCIANA
PALM BEACH
MR. H. E. BEMIS, Manager
January 16, 1928, to March 23, 1928
Per Day
Single room . . . . $12.00 to $14.00
Single room with bath . . . 16.00 to 22.00
Double room . . . . 24.00 to 28.00
Double room with bath . . . 28.00 to 34.00
American Plan.
Special Season Rates.

ALCAZAR
ST. AUGUSTINE
MR. JAMES K. HYDE, Manager
December 19, 1927, to March 31, 1928
Per Day
Single room . . . . $ 8.00 to $10.00
Single room with bath . . . 10.00 to 14.00
Double room . . . . 16.00 to 20.00
Double room with bath . . . 18.00 to 26.00
American Plan.

THE BREAKERS
PALM BEACH
MR. JOHN W. GREENE, Manager
December 14, 1927, to April 10, 1928
Per Day
Single room with bath . . $20.00 to $24.00
Double room with bath . . 30.00 to 40.00
American Plan.
Special Season Rates.

CORDOVA
ST. AUGUSTINE
MR. JAMES K. HYDE, Manager
December 19, 1927, to March 31, 1928
Per Day
Single room . . . . $ 3.00
Single room with bath . . . 4.00
Double room 4.00
Double room with bath . . . 5.00 to $ 8.00
European Plan.

ROYAL PALM
MIAMI
MR. JOSEPH P. GREAVES, Manager
December 31, 1927, to March 31, 1928
Per Day
Single room . . . . $12.00 to $14.00
Single room with bath . . . 16.00 to 20.00
Double room . . . . 24.00 to 24.00
Double room with bath . . . 30.00 to 32.00
American Plan.
Special Season Rates.

ORMOND
ORMOND-ON-THE-HALIFAX
MR. L. R. JOHNSTON, Manager
December 31, 1927, to April 2, 1928
Per Day
Single room . . . . $ 9.00 to $10.00
Single room with bath . . . 12.00 to 16.00
Double room . . . . 16.00 to 20.00
Double room with bath . . . 22.00 to 28.00
American Plan.

LONG KEY FISHING CAMP
LONG KEY
MR. GEORGE G. SCHUTT, Manager
December 24, 1927, to April 12, 1928
Per Day
Single room . . . . $ 7.00 to $10.00
Double room . . . . 13.00 to 18.00
American Plan.

CASA MARINA
KEY WEST
MR. L. P. SCHUTT, Manager
January 2, 1928, to March 31, 1928
Per Day
Single room with bath $11.00
Double room with bath $20.00
American Plan.

FLORIDA EAST COAST HOTEL COMPANY
FLAGLER SYSTEM

NEW YORK BOOKING OFFICE
2 WEST 45TH STREET

The hotel subsidiary of the Flagler System operated nine distinctive properties in 1928. If one craved high society, the place to stay was the Breakers in Palm Beach, where the best double room went for $40 a day.

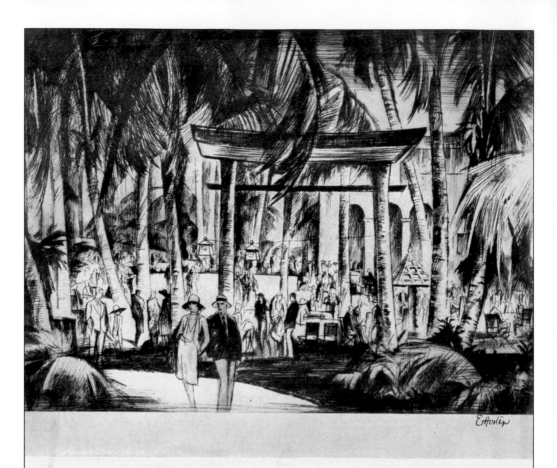

Where Shadows Play Through Dancing Palms

South . . . . and even farther south . . . . to the Gulf Stream and the Florida East Coast . . . . Ponce de Leon's land of eternal youth. . . . . follow the highway of the Florida East Coast Railway . . . . smoothly behind big oil burning locomotives . . . . cinderless and dustless to Palm Beach, Miami, St. Augustine . . . . the American Riviera.

THE MAGIC OF THE GULF STREAM

Golf on perfect fairways . . . . tennis . . . . polo . . . . bridle paths . . . . motor routes along the Coast . . . . bathing at summer temperature when winter grips the North . . . . dancing beneath the palms . . . . yachting in sheltered bays or open sea . . . . sailfish or tarpon . . . . and the famed hotels of the Flagler System.

Less than thirty hours from New York . . . . forty from Chicago . . . . on limited through trains . . . . for information write . . . .

FLORIDA EAST COAST

Railway and Hotel Companies

(Flagler System)

Operating the following hotels (American Plan)

General Offices St. Augustine, Fla.	Ponce de Leon . St. Augustine Alcazar . . . St. Augustine Cordova [European plan] St. Augustine Long Key Fishing Camp, Long Key	The Breakers . . Palm Beach Royal Poinciana . Palm Beach Hotel Ormond . . Ormond Casa Marina . . Key West	2 West 45th Street New York City

Seductive ads helped attract customers to the Flagler System. This one appeared in the November 1928 issue of *House & Garden* magazine. The Atlantic Coast Line and Seaboard Airline Railroads did not own hotel properties in Florida, though each served cities that boasted such. Thus, during the boom years, the FEC could both transport tourists and offer accommodations for every pocketbook.

The "East Coast of Florida" was another FEC publication that circulated during the boom. This one, which was released in 1926, had 50 pages of travel information, maps, and photos. Pastel colors graced the cover, along with a flapper playing golf.

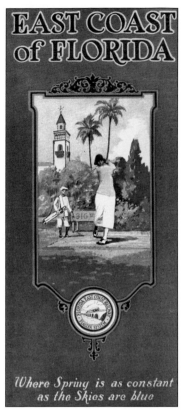

EAST COAST of FLORIDA

Where Spring is as constant as the Skies are blue

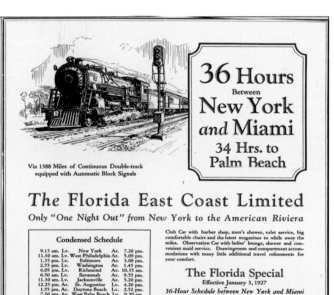

36 Hours
Between
New York
and Miami
34 Hrs. to
Palm Beach

Via 1388 Miles of Continuous Double-track equipped with Automatic Block Signals

The Florida East Coast Limited

Only "One Night Out" from New York to the American Riviera

Club Car with barber shop, men's shower, valet service, big comfortable chairs and the latest magazines to while away the miles. Observation Car with ladies' lounge, shower and convenient maid service. Drawingroom and compartment accommodations with many little additional travel refinements for your comfort.

Condensed Schedule

9.15 am. Lv.	New York	Ar.	7.20 pm.
11.30 am. Lv.	West Philadelphia	Ar.	5.09 pm.
1.35 pm. Lv.	Baltimore	Ar.	3.00 pm.
2.55 pm. Lv.	Washington	Ar.	1.45 pm.
6.05 pm. Lv.	Richmond	Ar.	10.35 am.
6.50 pm. Lv.	Savannah	Ar.	9.55 am.
11.30 am. Lv.	Jacksonville	Ar.	5.20 pm.
12.25 pm. Ar.	St. Augustine	Lv.	4.20 pm.
1.55 pm. Ar.	Daytona Beach	Lv.	2.52 pm.
7.30 pm. Ar.	West Palm Beach	Lv.	9.20 am.
9.30 pm. Ar.	Miami	Lv.	7.20 am.

The Florida Special

Effective January 3, 1927

36-Hour Schedule between New York and Miami

Identical in service and equipment with that of the Florida East Coast Limited

FLORIDA EAST COAST RAILWAY

FLAGLER SYSTEM

Complete Double-track
Oil-Burning Locomotives—*No Cinders*

Automatic Block Signals
Rock-Ballasted Roadbed — *No Dust*

NEW YORK OFFICE
2 West 45th Street

GENERAL OFFICES
St. Augustine, Fla.

The Florida East Coast Limited traversed the Pennsylvania Railroad between New York and Washington. The Richmond, Fredericksburg & Potomac took charge to Richmond, whereupon the Atlantic Coast Line hauled it to Jacksonville. Then the FEC advanced the crack train to Miami.

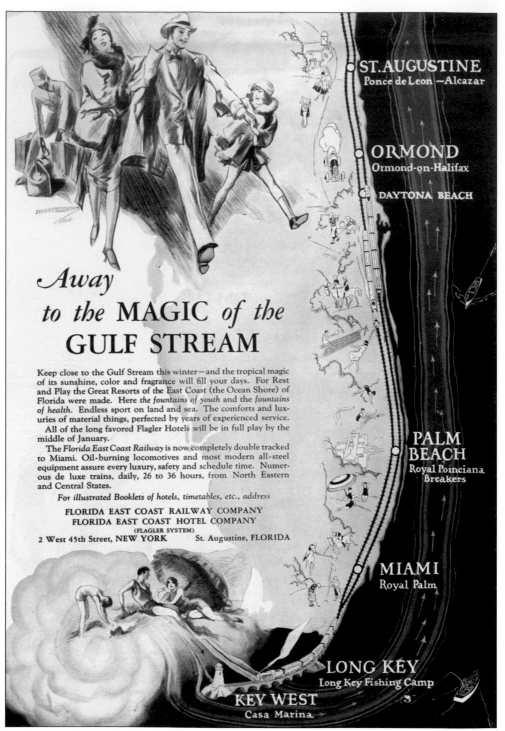

Away to the MAGIC of the GULF STREAM

Keep close to the Gulf Stream this winter—and the tropical magic of its sunshine, color and fragrance will fill your days. For Rest and Play the Great Resorts of the East Coast (the Ocean Shore) of Florida were made. Here *the fountains of youth* and the *fountains of health.* Endless sport on land and sea. The comforts and luxuries of material things, perfected by years of experienced service.

All of the long favored Flagler Hotels will be in full play by the middle of January.

The *Florida East Coast Railway* is now completely double tracked to Miami. Oil-burning locomotives and most modern all-steel equipment assure every luxury, safety and schedule time. Numerous de luxe trains, daily, 26 to 36 hours, from North Eastern and Central States.

For illustrated Booklets of hotels, timetables, etc., address

FLORIDA EAST COAST RAILWAY COMPANY
FLORIDA EAST COAST HOTEL COMPANY
(FLAGLER SYSTEM)
2 West 45th Street, NEW YORK   **St. Augustine, FLORIDA**

ST. AUGUSTINE
Ponce de Leon — Alcazar

ORMOND
Ormond-on-Halifax

DAYTONA BEACH

PALM BEACH
Royal Poinciana
Breakers

MIAMI
Royal Palm

LONG KEY
Long Key Fishing Camp

KEY WEST
Casa Marina

Coaxing travelers to the Flagler System was a never-ending task. Here a family of three is first seen dashing to the train, only to re-appear on a sandy beach. This ad appeared in the January 1927 issue of *The Spur*—an upscale magazine long since defunct. But the Florida East Coast Railway still lives on!

Two

HERE COMES THE 'COAST LINE

For decades, the Atlantic Coast Line Railroad (ACL) played an important role in the transportation affairs of six Southeastern states. In 1920, the company owned assets totaling $318.2 million. It operated 4,900 miles of track—1,793 in Florida—a figure that grew to 13,333 miles when controlling interests in other railroads were factored. The company's mainline stretched between Richmond, Virginia, and Jacksonville. When the boom began, some 10 million passengers were being conveyed over the ACL system together with 17.3 million tons of freight. Nearly 25,000 workers were on the payroll.

Ever since its founding, the ACL undertook system-wide expansion and improvement projects. The 1920 initiatives in Florida included the laying of new steel rail, enlarging the freight yard at Lakeland, and erecting new stations at Lake Wales, Frostproof, Avon Park, and Richland. Shop improvements were also completed at Sanford and High Springs. Further work progressed on two important taproots: the Haines City Branch and the Tampa Southern Railroad.

The Haines City Branch, which departed the ACL mainline at Haines City, proceeded down the central ridge district of Florida, an area known for citrus and vegetable production, mining, and lumbering. Service to Sebring started in June 1912. Later management approved extending the line to Immokalee (by way of Harrisburg and Goodno) along with a spur from Harrisburg to Moore Haven, on the western tip of Lake Okeechobee, the latter opening in 1918. Work on the main stem continued to Goodno (1919), whereupon the project halted owing to wartime retrenchments. However, work resumed in 1920, and biweekly train service to Immokalee began the following year.

Chartered in 1917, the Tampa Southern Railroad was to tap the agricultural traffic of Manatee County and connect Tampa with Sarasota. From its inception, the company forged a close relationship with the ACL, the latter having purchased its entire stock issue. The Tampa Southern track departed the ACL mainline at Uceta (east of Tampa) and was completed to Gillett and Palmetto in 1919. To obtain phosphate traffic east of Palmetto, the company constructed the Ellenton Belt Line, an inland loop of track between Gillett and Palmetto by way of Seth, which opened in 1921. In the previous year, the Tampa Southern main line was opened to Bradenton along with a spur off the Ellenton Belt Line to Senanky.

As boom fever spread, the ACL's presence in Florida grew. In 1924, the Tampa Southern reached Sarasota. Farther down the Gulf coast was Fort Myers. The ACL already served that community, but area business leaders wanted service extended south of the "City of Palms" to Bonita Springs, Naples, and Collier City (Marco Island). In fact, they obtained a charter for the Fort Myers Southern Railroad. The ACL acquired the paper company, and soon construction crews were in the field.

The Fort Myers Southern was opened to Bonita Springs in 1925, whereupon workers started to advance the line down to Naples. That year, the ACL also acquired and built the Moore Haven & Clewiston Railroad so as to obtain area sugar cane and vegetable traffic in the region. Construction also resumed on the Haines City Branch south of Immokalee to Deep Lake, where advertising magnate Barron Collier (of Collier County fame) owned groves of grapefruit. Also ACL management decided to extend the Tampa Southern beyond Sarasota to Southfort (Fort Ogden), where the line would intercept the Lakeland–Fort Myers route. The most significant project begun that year was the Perry Cut-off between Perry and Monticello and from Thonotosassa to Richland. When completed, the shortcut would form a convenient artery for traffic moving between Tampa and the Midwest by way of Thomasville and Albany, Georgia.

These various endeavors were all in response to the land boom. As ACL chairman Henry Walters noted in the 1925 annual report: "Your Company has watched the rapid growth of Florida and has anticipated the transportation needs of the State by substantial improvements to your property. No one, however, could have foreseen the phenomenal growth and development that has taken place there in less than a year's time, thrusting suddenly upon the railroad such a volume of business that it was unable to give normal service." The same report discloses that the ACL enjoyed record revenues that year—$93.9 million.

The boom lost ground in 1926 as real estate buyers began to vanish. Nevertheless the ACL that year inaugurated service between Sarasota and Eutopia, Bonita Springs and Naples, and from Immokalee to Deep Lake. Further a huge yard and shop complex was begun at Uceta (near Tampa), where over 1,000 persons would one day be employed. Revenues that year reached another record: $97 million.

In 1927, the long-awaited Perry Cutoff opened for freight service, the Tampa Southern reached Southfort, the Fort Myers Southern opened to Collier City (Marco Island), and the Haines City Branch was fast approaching Deep Lake. Unfortunately revenues fell to $80 million. Another drop was recorded in 1928, which prompted management to cut expenses and defer maintenance. Despite the retrenchments, service to Deep Lake was started, the government allowed the ACL to purchase the Deep Lake Railroad (owned by Barron Collier) between Deep Lake and Everglades, the Moore Haven & Clewiston Railway was extended to Canal Point so as to serve another mill of Southern Sugar Company, and passenger trains now began using the Perry Cut-off. Interestingly the ACL sold a Florida asset in 1928: its 51-percent stake in the Live Oak, Perry & Gulf Railroad (Live Oak to Flint Rock), though close relations with that firm continued.

In 1929, the ACL rebuilt Barron Collier's little railroad between Deep Lake and Everglades, whereupon service to that remote hamlet was initiated. In fact, Everglades became the southernmost point of the entire Atlantic Coast Line Railroad. And on that note, our brief look at this important carrier during the boom comes to a close.

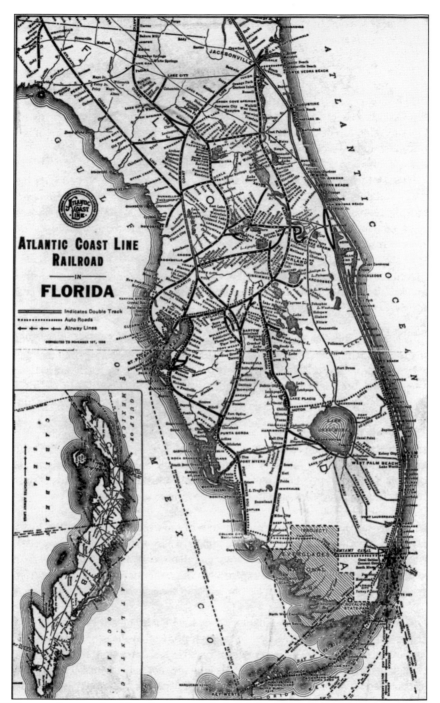

This 1928 map depicts the Florida routes of the Atlantic Coast Line Railroad. The latter obtained a presence below Charleston, South Carolina, in 1903 by purchasing the Plant System of Railroads for $28 million. The ACL penetrated the central and southwest sections of Florida, including Tampa, where Henry Plant erected the palatial Tampa Bay Hotel. Even though the Atlantic Coast Line Railroad expanded the former Plant System in Florida, the empire was caught unprepared for the tidal wave of boom traffic.

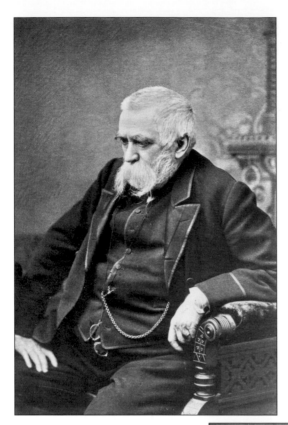

The wealthy Baltimore merchant William Walters formed an alliance of Southern railroads after the Civil War that ultimately became the Atlantic Coast Line system. He sought to get early vegetables to northern markets and transport winter-weary tourists to a warm clime. (Courtesy Walters Art Museum, Baltimore.)

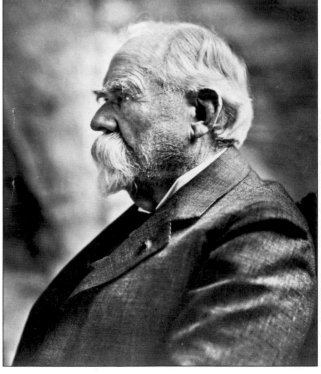

Henry Walters, son of William, was appointed general manager of the ACL syndicate in 1884. Later he became its president, chairman, and principal stockholder. Enormously wealthy, he loved fine art, European travel, and yachts. The Florida land boom amazed him and every other ACL executive. (Courtesy Walters Art Museum, Baltimore.)

The *Florida Special* was the ACL's flagship passenger train. It was conceived in 1887 by Henry Walters, who got car builder George Pullman to finance construction. It was enhanced through the years, and during the boom, it did a land-office business.

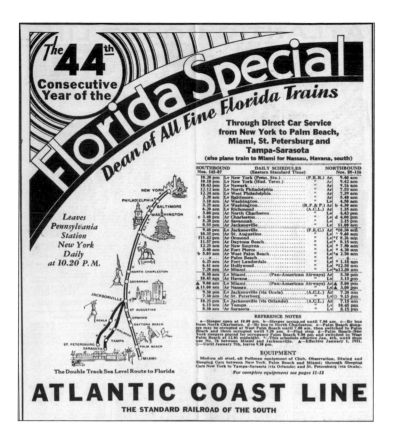

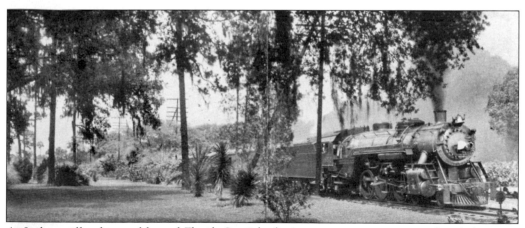

At Jacksonville, the southbound *Florida Special* split into two sections: one was handed over to the FEC for the trip to Miami; the other sped over ACL tracks to sunny St. Petersburg. Here she is on home rails "smoking it up" near Ocala in 1926.

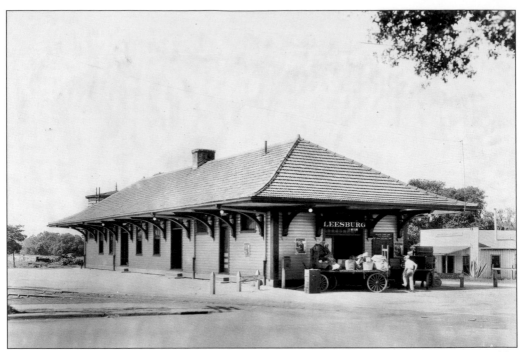

The ACL station at Leesburg (below Ocala) appears busy in this 1926 scene. It was snapped by Burgert Brothers, photographers of Tampa. Tourists still revel in the region's lakes, fishing, and hunting. (Courtesy Tampa–Hillsborough County Public Library.)

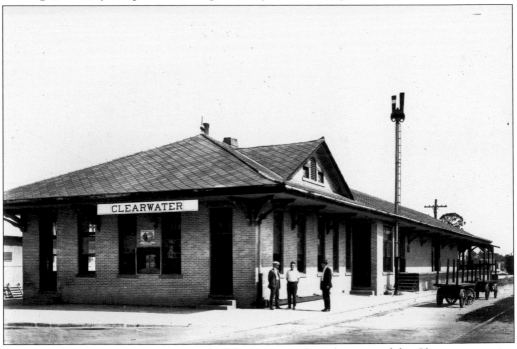

Burgert Brothers made a lasting record of the boom, such as this view of the Clearwater station in 1927. Not far from here, a spur track brought guests to the majestic Belleview Hotel, which Henry Plant opened in 1897. (Courtesy Tampa–Hillsborough County Public Library.)

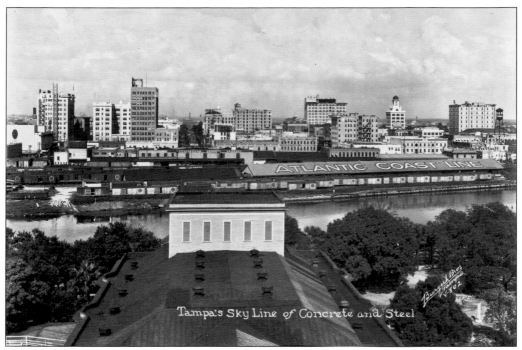

Tampa's Sky Line of Concrete and Steel

How much the ACL dominated Tampa's Hillsborough River is obvious in this 1920s image. To compose the photograph, a Burgert Brothers staffer stood in Plant Park, on the grounds of the famous Tampa Bay Hotel. (Courtesy Tampa–Hillsborough County Public Library.)

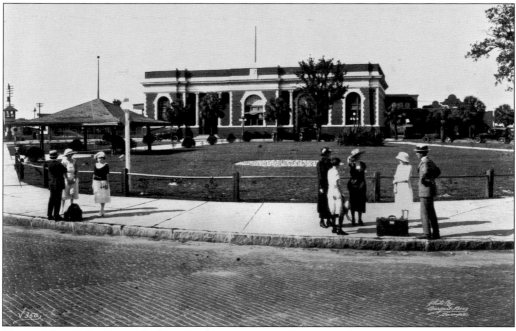

Tampa Union Station, which opened in 1912, was built of reddish-brown brick, terra cotta, and light-colored stone. The Beaux Arts structure was jointly owned by the ACL and the Seaboard Air Line Railway. This image was made in 1928. (Courtesy Tampa–Hillsborough County Public Library.)

A popular ACL train during the boom was *The Pinellas Special*, which ran between Jacksonville and beautiful St. Petersburg. As this 1927 timetable reveals, the train even serviced the spur to the historic Belleview-Biltmore Hotel.

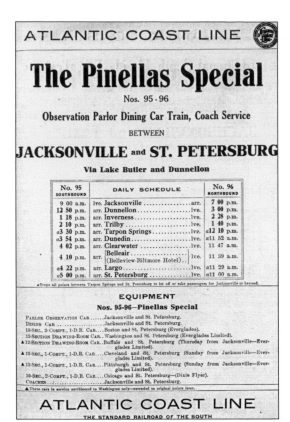

ATLANTIC COAST LINE

The Pinellas Special
Nos. 95-96

Observation Parlor Dining Car Train, Coach Service
BETWEEN

JACKSONVILLE and ST. PETERSBURG
Via Lake Butler and Dunnellon

No. 95 SOUTHBOUND	DAILY SCHEDULE	No. 96 NORTHBOUND
9 00 a.m.	lve. Jacksonville ....arr.	7 00 p.m.
12 50 p.m.	arr. Dunnellon ....lve.	3 00 p.m.
1 18 p.m.	arr. Inverness ....lve.	2 28 p.m.
2 10 p.m.	arr. Trilby ....lve.	1 40 p.m.
a3 30 p.m.	arr. Tarpon Springs ....lve.	a12 10 p.m.
a3 54 p.m.	arr. Dunedin ....lve.	a11 52 a.m.
4 02 p.m.	arr. Clearwater ....lve.	11 47 a.m.
4 10 p.m.	arr. {Belleair .... (Belleview-Biltmore Hotel).. } lve.	11 39 a.m.
a4 22 p.m.	arr. Largo ....lve.	a11 29 a.m.
a5 00 p.m.	arr. St. Petersburg ....lve.	a11 00 a.m.

a Stops all points between Tarpon Springs and St. Petersburg to let off or take passengers for Jacksonville or beyond.

EQUIPMENT
Nos. 95-96—Pinellas Special

PARLOR OBSERVATION CAR......Jacksonville and St. Petersburg.
DINING CAR ....Jacksonville and St. Petersburg.
10-SEC., 2-COMPT., 1-D.R. CAR....Boston and St. Petersburg (Everglades).
13-SECTION DRAWING-ROOM CAR..Washington and St. Petersburg (Everglades Limited).
▲12-SECTION DRAWING-ROOM CAR....Buffalo and St. Petersburg (Thursday from Jacksonville—Everglades Limited).
▲12-SEC., 1-COMPT., 1-D.R. CAR....Cleveland and St. Petersburg (Sunday from Jacksonville—Everglades Limited).
▲12-SEC., 1-COMPT., 1-D.R. CAR....Pittsburgh and St. Petersburg (Sunday from Jacksonville—Everglades Limited).
10-SEC., 2-COMPT., 1-D.R. CAR....Chicago and St. Petersburg—(Dixie Flyer).
COACHES..................Jacksonville and St. Petersburg.
▲ These cars in service northbound to Washington only—extended to original points later.

ATLANTIC COAST LINE
THE STANDARD RAILROAD OF THE SOUTH

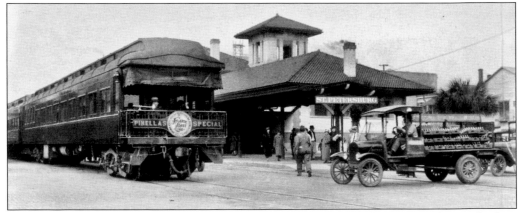

The Pinellas Special is ready to depart St. Petersburg for Jacksonville. The parlor car had an observation deck and chairs, though dust and cinders were not unknown. A Ford truck lumbers over the crossing with cases of that immortal elixir—Coca-Cola.

ATLANTIC COAST LINE RAILROAD— HAINES CITY BRANCH
Haines City to Everglades

Station	Miles	Station	Miles	Station	Miles
Haines City	0.0	Avon Park	38.5	Goodno	100.4
Prine	3.0	Sebring	46.3	Sears	110.4
Lake Hamilton	5.2	DeSoto City	50.6	Keri	113.7
Leco	5.9	Istopoga	55.1	Felda	118.6
Dundee	6.8	Lake Placid	62.9	Immokalee	126.1
Waverly	9.8	View	67.8	Bunker Hill	129.0
Mountain Lake	11.4	Childs	68.8	Harker	133.2
Lake Wales	15.3	Hicora	73.6	Sunniland	138.6
Highland Park	17.2	Venus	79.5	Miles City	146.4
Babson Park	21.3	Palmdale	88.3	Deep Lake	154.0
Frostproof	27.8	Harrisburg	89.4	Copeland	160.7
Pittsburg	34.5	Hall City	93.1	Carnestown	163.1
Aro	36.6	Ortona	98.0	Everglades	167.1

Harrisburg to Lake Harbor

Station	Miles	Station	Miles	Station	Miles
Harrisburg	0.0	Cobert	17.1	Gunson	25.7
Muckway	9.8	Roumania	18.1	Sugartown	26.8
New Hall	14.3	Benbow	19.7	Highway Spur	27.6
Moore Haven	15.7	Frierson	21.7	Clewiston	30.8
Caspur	16.1	Capar	22.5	Lakeside	34.8
Gram	16.6	Liberty Point	22.7	Lake Harbor	41.0

This chart enumerates every station on the ACL's Haines City Branch together with the spur to Moore Haven and Lake Harbor. Everglades City had the distinction of being the southernmost point on the entire ACL system.

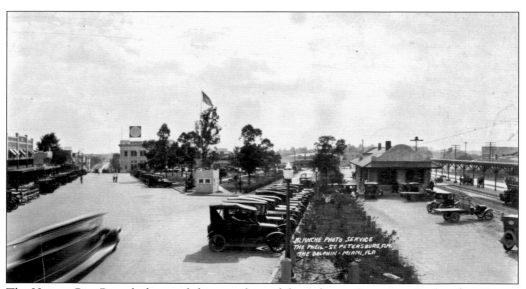

The Haines City Branch departed the main line of the Atlantic Coast Line Railroad at Haines City. The setting was named for Plant System superintendent Henry Haines, a New Englander by birth who served the Confederate railroad cause. The branch passed through the so-called "Scenic Highlands" of Florida.

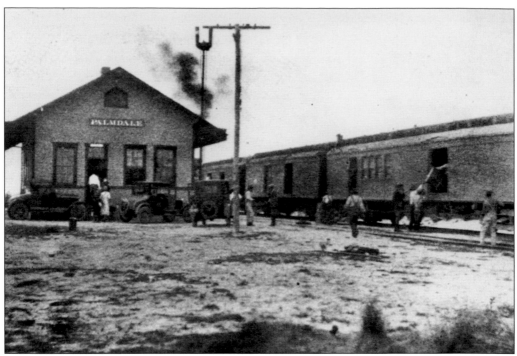

Palmdale flourished during the boom. Area waterways and forests attracted sportsmen. Business appears to be good in this 1921 scene. Freight and mail is being unloaded from the baggage car.

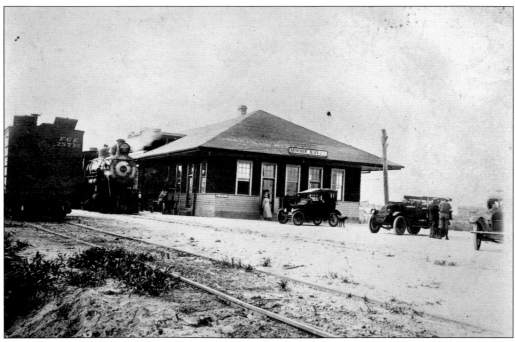

The rich muck lands at Moore Haven produced bumper crops of vegetables, which were then shipped to northern markets via ACL trains. A ventilated boxcar for perishables can be seen at far left.

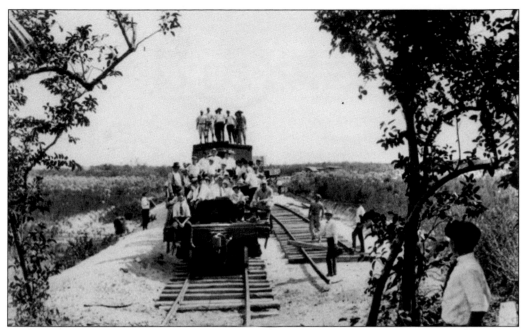

The first ACL train gingerly rolled into Clewiston on September 7, 1921. Celebrants sat on flat cars or stood atop boxcars. Sugar cane was grown and processed here by Southern Sugar Company, which erected several mills.

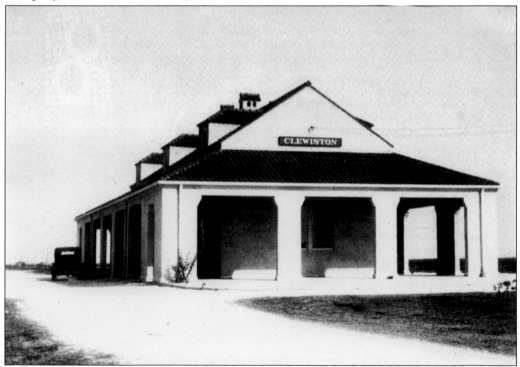

Clewiston received a handsome station in the Spanish style, replete with bell tower. The building was constructed of concrete block covered with white stucco. The roof was comprised of bright-red tiles. The overhangs shaded passengers from the hot Florida sun.

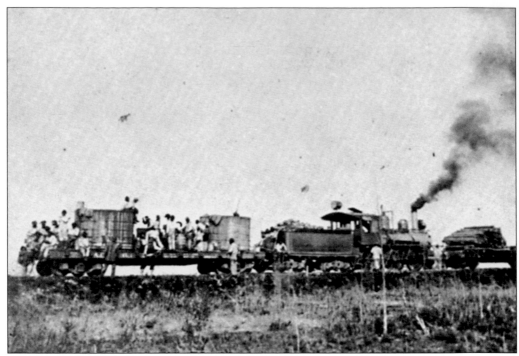

At first, railway operations into the Moore Haven–Clewiston area were primitive at best. Often the poor and down-trodden hitched rides on this slow-moving consist, which was nicknamed *The Hinky-Dink*. Passengers jumped off whenever so motivated.

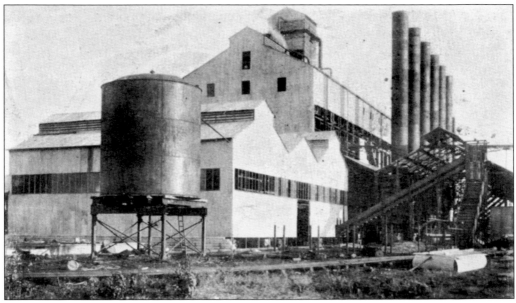

The major ACL customer at Clewiston was the Southern Sugar Company. At its Clewiston mill, pictured here, cane went in, processed sugar and molasses came out.

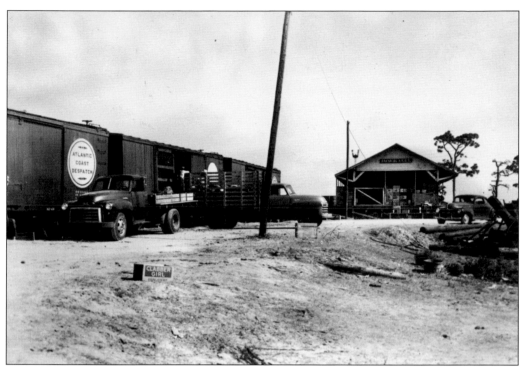

A burgeoning agricultural and timber industry sprung up around Immokalee. Here workers are loading kegs and crates of vegetables into ventilated boxcars owned by Atlantic Coast Despatch—an ACL subsidiary.

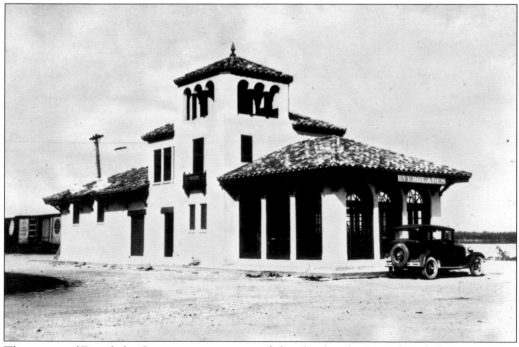

This image of Everglades City station was snapped shortly after the Spanish-styled structure was completed. Today parts of the building help form a popular local restaurant.

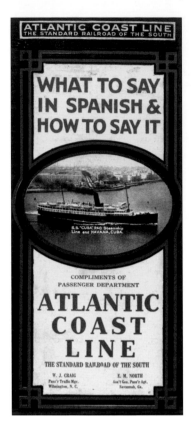

Many ACL passengers departed Florida for Havana and other tropical destinations. To assist with the language barrier, this 32-page guide was prepared by the ACL in 1923. It was freely distributed and proved to be a very popular publication.

During the boom, the ACL issued a series of small brochures entitled "Timely Railroad Topics." Each number addressed some issue that confronted the ACL or the railroad industry as a whole. The goal was to create public support.

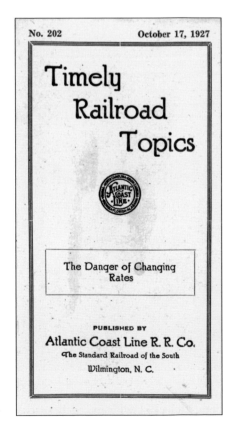

A trip aboard the famous *Havana Special* was not easily forgotten, primarily because part of the journey was made over the famous Key West Extension of the Florida East Coast Railway. Passengers detrained at Key West then boarded a boat for Havana.

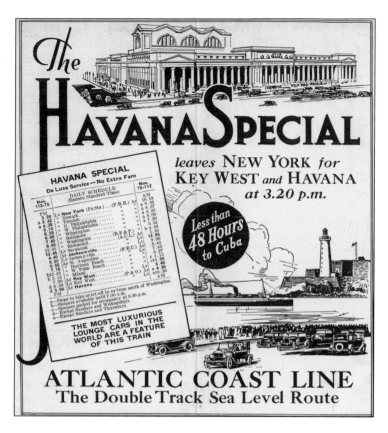

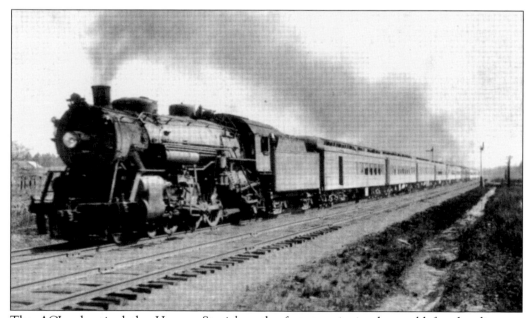

The ACL advertised the *Havana Special* as the fastest train in the world for the distance traversed. Here it is dashing past Callahan, Florida, on March 9, 1926. The ACL mainline between Jacksonville and Richmond was double-tracked and immaculately maintained.

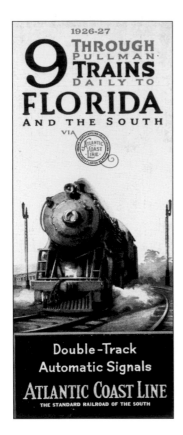

At the boom's height, the ACL operated nine separate Pullman trains between New York and Florida. Another group of nine serviced the Midwest, again in conjunction with other railroads. Never again was such frequency of service offered to the Sunshine State.

Like the FEC, the ACL issued attractive brochures and booklets during the boom. Perhaps its most popular publication was "Tropical Trips." Every resort and point of interest along the ACL route was detailed. Fabulous photos also helped to tell the story.

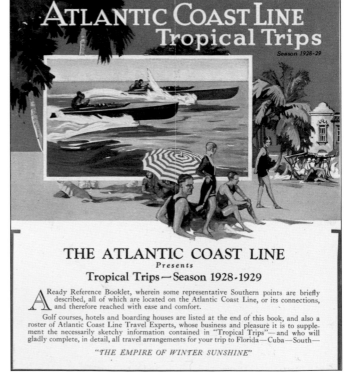

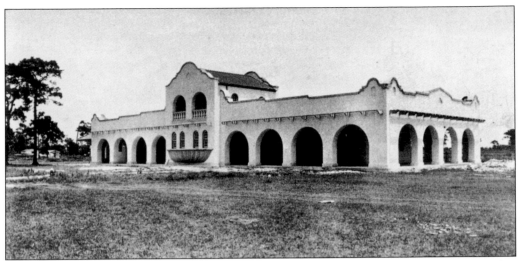

Many new stations were built by the ACL during the 1920s. This Spanish structure is what Sarasota received. It was designed in-house by an ACL architect at company headquarters in Wilmington, North Carolina. A virtual twin was erected at Fort Myers that, unlike Sarasota, still survives.

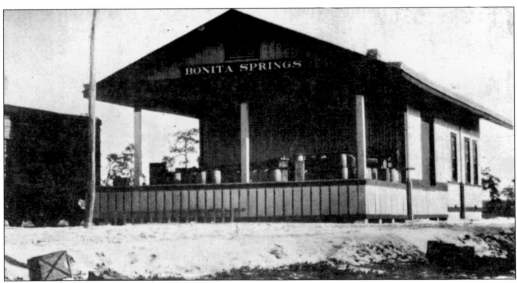

Not so elegant was the wood-frame station built at Bonita Springs, below Fort Myers. In this 1928 scene, crates of vegetables and citrus crowd the freight platform. During the boom, the Seaboard Air Line Railway built a parallel line through this part of the world.

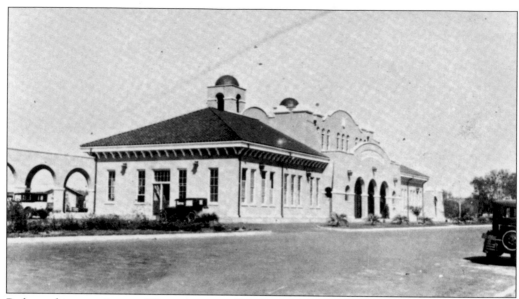

Perhaps the preeminent edifice constructed by the ACL during the 1920s was the new passenger station at Orlando on Sligh Boulevard. It was conceived in the Spanish Colonial style and completed in 1927. In recent years, it has been thoughtfully restored.

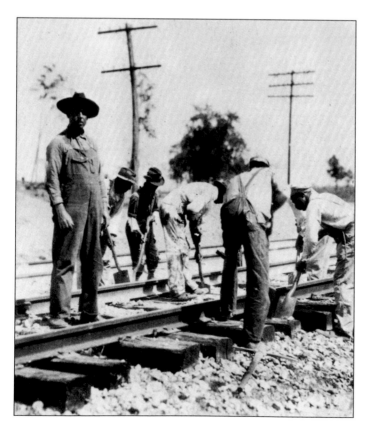

Track workers have played an overlooked yet indispensable role in Florida railroad history. This African American crew on the ACL near Tampa toils away while their foreman looks at the camera. The work was not for the faint of heart.

One of the biggest and costliest boom-era railroad projects in Florida was the ACL's Perry Cut-off. When completed, it provided a handy artery for traffic moving between Tampa–St. Petersburg and the Midwest. (Courtesy Russell Tedder.)

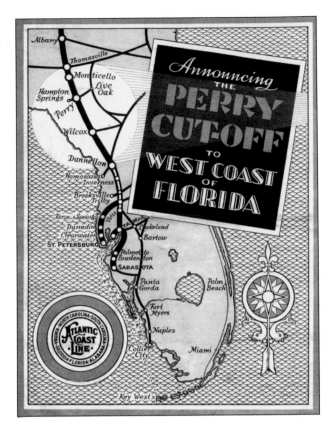

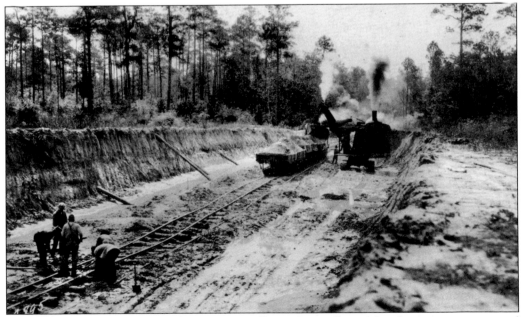

Steam shovels clamor away on the Perry Cut-off near Dunnellon. After the route was surveyed and grubbed, excavation and grading took place along with bridge building. Then cross ties and tie plates were positioned, followed by the spiking of steel rails.

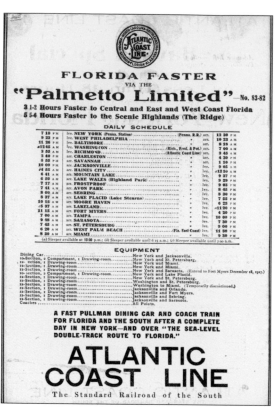

The *Palmetto Limited* serviced the Haines City Branch to Moore Haven, as this 1927 timetable reveals. Connecting service was also offered to Fort Myers, Tampa, Sarasota, and to east coast points via the Florida East Coast Railway.

Another popular ACL train was the *Tampa Special*, which ran between Tampa and Jacksonville. In this 1929 view, it is about to depart Tampa Union Station. The straw boater, which the passenger is waving, has also vanished.

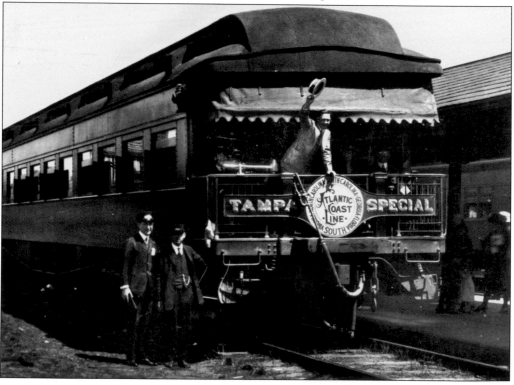

Three

WARFIELD AND
THE SEABOARD

The Seaboard Air Line Railway ("Seaboard") was smaller than the Atlantic Coast Line, yet it served practically the same territory. When the Florida land boom began in 1920, the Seaboard owned assets worth $244.2 million, including some 3,500 miles of track, 1,036 in Florida. About six million passengers were transported over the railway that year along with 12.9 million tons of freight. The company's aggressive chairman and president was Baltimore banker S. Davies Warfield, who had obtained a stock majority in 1912.

Warfield's keen interest in Florida started long before the boom itself. Often he would praise the potentials of the state, citing its favorable climate and industrious people. He also predicted a great future for its citrus and phosphate industries. His boon companion during the boom was Florida governor John Martin. Warfield would often appear at Florida events with the state's chief executive at his side.

The Seaboard dramatically expanded in Florida in the 1920s. Warfield's vision for the state was articulated in the company's 1924 annual report. That year, Warfield organized the Florida Western & Northern Railroad, whose track would depart the Seaboard mainline at Coleman (below Wildwood) and head for West Palm Beach. Other initiatives included the Gross-Callahan Cut-off (it allowed time-sensitive trains to bypass busy Jacksonville) and the Valrico Cut-off, which, in conjunction with other Seaboard tracks, would connect both coasts of the state.

Warfield's expansionary measures reached an even greater crescendo in 1925. New terminal facilities were built at Baldwin and Wildwood, heavier steel rail was installed between Waldo and Inverness, and seven miles of double track were activated between Baldwin and Waldo. That year, Warfield personally opened the new line into West Palm Beach using four separate sections of the newly christened *Orange Blossom Special* passenger train. Also Seaboard trains began using the Gross-Callahan and Valrico Cutoffs. Further the company leased the East & West Coast Railway between Arcadia and Manatee along with the Tampa Northern Railroad, which offered freight and passenger service from Tampa to Brooksville and Tooke

Lake. Warfield also had an annoying gap filled in between the Florida cities of Brooksville and Inverness. Further the Interstate Commerce Commission approved the Seaboard's lease and purchase of the Charlotte Harbor & Northern Railway, a prosperous hauler of phosphate whose track ran down from Mulberry to Arcadia, Hull, and to the company's huge marine terminal in South Boca Grande.

If these endeavors were not enough, the ICC also approved one more Warfield project in 1925: the Seaboard All-Florida Railway. This subsidiary would advance Seaboard rails south of West Palm Beach to Miami and Florida City, and permit construction of a new extension down the Gulf coast from Hull to Fort Myers and Bonita together with lateral branches at Fort Myers to LaBelle and Punta Rassa. Another leased entity—the Naples, Seaboard & Gulf Railway—would advance the extension south of Bonita to Naples proper. Warfield foresaw a great future for the lower Gulf coast. Huge stands of virgin timber existed here, and parts of the territory already supported a large citrus and vegetable business. Further Warfield wished to develop Naples and Punta Rassa into deepwater ports. The Interstate Commerce Commission (ICC) approved all of Warfield's requests, but one commissioner—the distinguished public servant George Eastman—opposed every Seaboard expansion, stating that the territories were already provided with railroad transportation and that the financial cost to the Seaboard could eventually overwhelm the company. Eastman was out-voted by his fellow commissioners, though his forecast was later validated.

Financially 1926 was the Seaboard's best year of the decade. Revenues hit $67 million, while $3.1 million was recorded in net income. During the year, construction of the east and west coast extensions proceeded at breakneck speed. Also the company's mainline was double tracked between Baldwin and Starke, from Wildwood to Coleman, and for several miles near Tampa. The Seaboard also purchased the Tavares & Gulf Railroad, which served Florida's Lake County, a region noted for its beautiful lakes and citrus production.

Warfield opened the east and west coast extensions on January 7, 1927, in the presence of some 700 guests from 90 cities and 18 states. He pampered them aboard five separate sections of the *Orange Blossom Special*. Public ovations were tendered at every stop. Perhaps 20,000 Floridians witnessed the two-day event, which remains one of the most remarkable celebrations in American railroad history.

Other Seaboard endeavors that year included the leasing of the Tampa & Gulf Coast Railroad, whose track connected Tampa with St. Petersburg, Tarpon Springs, and New Port Richey. Additionally, the Seaboard acquired the Jacksonville, Gainesville & Gulf Railway, which operated between Emathla, Gainesville, and Sampson City—the so-called "Fruit and Vegetable Route of Florida." The Seaboard's branch between Fort Myers and LaBelle opened in 1927 as well as the line from Hialeah to Homestead. Additionally, the company started to install automatic block signals between Baldwin and Coleman. Unfortunately, Seaboard revenues fell in 1927 largely because the land boom was over. In fact, after all expenses were paid, the company earned a paltry $31,576 in net income! In October, the company suffered a major loss: the indefatigable S. Davies Warfield died in a Baltimore hospital.

The Seaboard produced mixed results for the rest of the decade. Another drop in revenues occurred in 1928, though by controlling expenses, an uptick in net income was reported. That year, the Seaboard leased the Georgia, Florida & Alabama Railroad (Richland, Georgia, to Carabelle, Florida). In 1930, a loss of $4.5 million was recorded. The large debt load the railway carried was becoming unbearable, just as ICC commissioner Joseph Eastman predicted. When Seaboard directors failed to find a solution, the company slipped into receivership, where it remained until the 1940s.

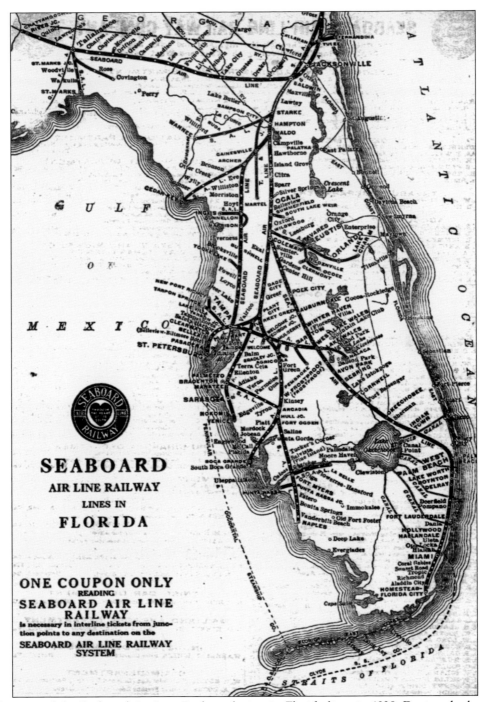

This map of the Seaboard Air Line Railway depicts its Florida lines in 1928. During the boom, Seaboard president S. Davies Warfield greatly expanded the railway's presence in the Sunshine State. In fact, some of the projects infuriated its competitors. For example, its line below West Palm Beach broke the monopoly of the Florida East Coast Railway. No wonder, the Seaboard was regarded as an interloper.

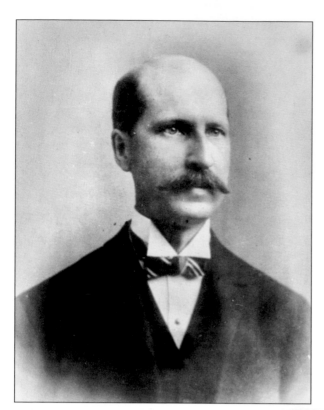

Solomon Davies Warfield was both chairman and president of the Seaboard during the 1920s. He had a deep regard for Florida, and his faith in the state was unshakable. A banker by reputation, he was also the Seaboard's major stockholder. He died in 1927.

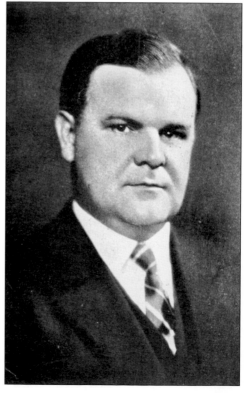

Florida governor John Martin admired Warfield's expansionary measures. A lawyer by training, Martin was mayor of Jacksonville for three terms. During the 1940s, he was first a co-receiver and later trustee of the Florida East Coast Railway.

Promoting the Seaboard Railway through literature never let up, especially in the busy 1920s. This booklet described industry and business opportunities within the Sunshine State. Copies were widely distributed, or they could be obtained by writing headquarters.

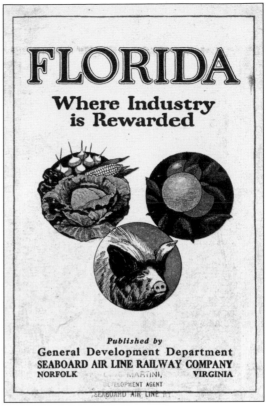

FLORIDA

Where Industry is Rewarded

Published by
General Development Department
SEABOARD AIR LINE RAILWAY COMPANY
NORFOLK   ~~MARTINI,~~   **VIRGINIA**
DEVELOPMENT AGENT
SEABOARD AIR LINE R[...]

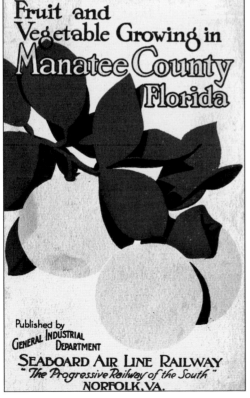

Fruit and Vegetable Growing in Manatee County Florida

Published by
GENERAL INDUSTRIAL DEPARTMENT
SEABOARD AIR LINE RAILWAY
"The Progressive Railway of the South"
NORFOLK, VA.

The Seaboard Railway reached the rich agricultural lands of Manatee County long before the ACL did with its Tampa Southern subsidiary. This interesting booklet was prepared for prospective growers and described everything from soil fertility to shipping methods.

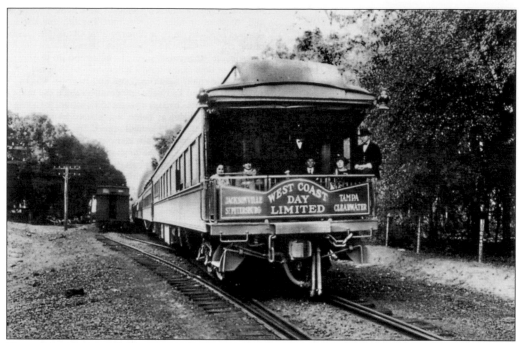

One of the Seaboard's more popular trains was the *West Coast Day Limited*, which serviced the Jacksonville–Tampa–St. Petersburg corridor. In this 1927 image, it is overtaking a freight train halted on the siding.

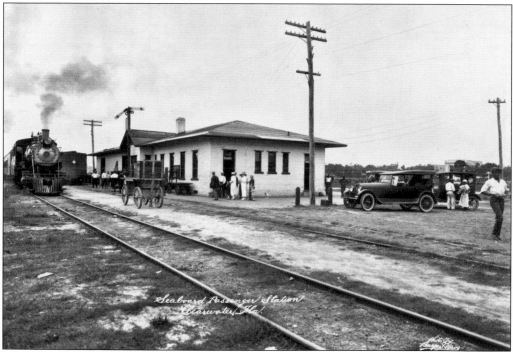

A Burgert Brothers photographer composed this classic setting of the Seaboard station at Clearwater in 1926. A train steams into town, passengers are mingling about the platform, while private "motorcars" stand at the ready. (Courtesy Tampa–Hillsborough County Public Library.)

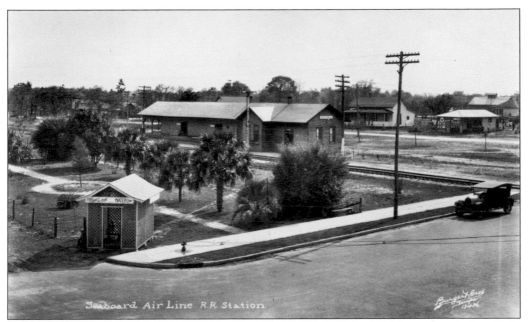

A somewhat pastoral setting greeted the Burgert Brothers photographer at the Zephyr Hills station. Afterward the artisan may have stepped into the booth in the left foreground and had a "free" glass of spring water, for which the town was famous. (Courtesy Tampa–Hillsborough County Public Library.)

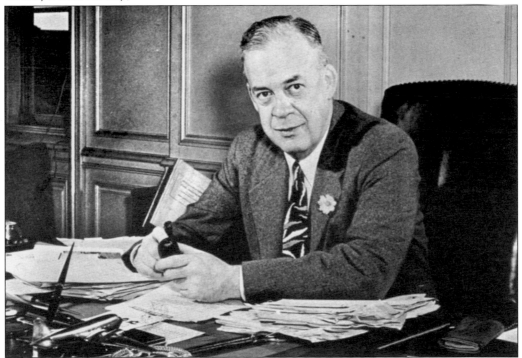

The Interstate Commerce Commission had to approve every Seaboard expansion plan in Florida. One commissioner, Joseph Eastman, deeply opposed all the projects as being unnecessary. He was outvoted. (Courtesy Railway and Locomotive Historical Society.)

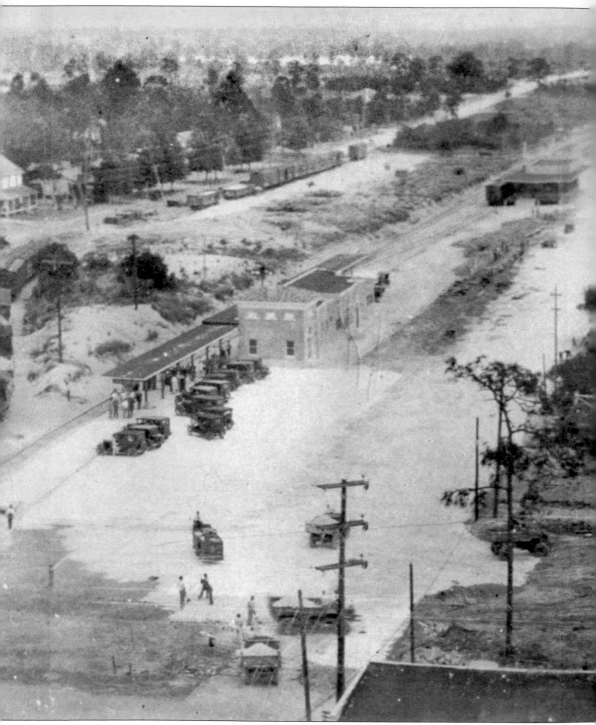

The Seaboard's important extension from Coleman (below Wildwood) to West Palm Beach passed through Avon Park, which was already served by the Atlantic Coast Line Railroad. To compose this 1926 view, which looks north, the photographer climbed atop a water tower. At bottom right is the ACL station and small yard at Avon Park. The newly constructed Seaboard

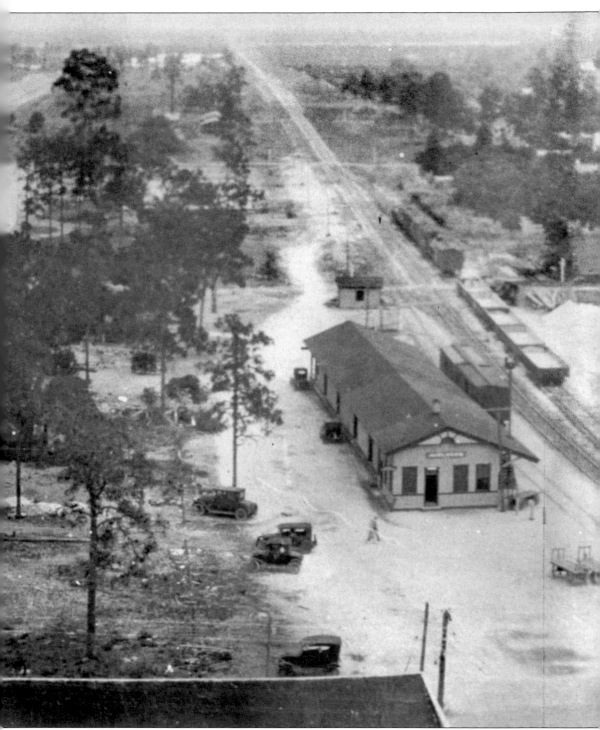

station can be seen at far left, surrounded with automobiles. The ACL station is gone, but CSX and Amtrak trains zip by the restored Seaboard station, which also houses a museum.

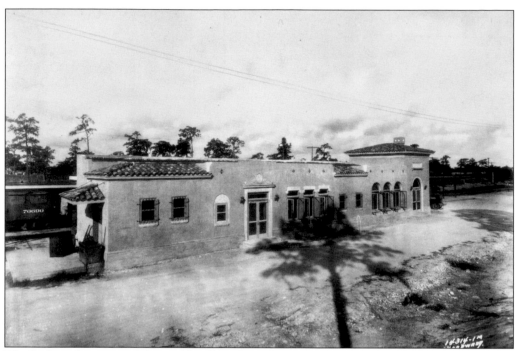

The Seaboard station at Sebring, like all on the Coleman–West Palm Beach route, was conceived by Harvey and Clarke, architects of West Palm Beach. It too has survived the sands of time and is used by Amtrak.

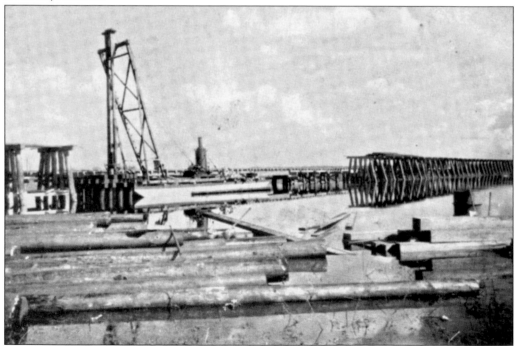

At the insistence of President Warfield, the Coleman–West Palm Beach line was rushed to completion by a South Carolina construction firm. This image was taken at the Kissimmee River crossing, near Fort Bassinger.

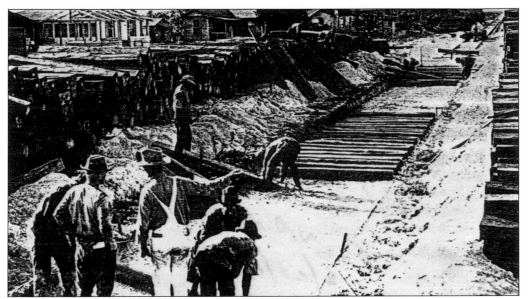

By June 1924, workers were positioning cross ties in West Palm Beach. Afterward tie plates and the steel rails were spiked. The man in white coveralls—the construction foreman—is barking orders.

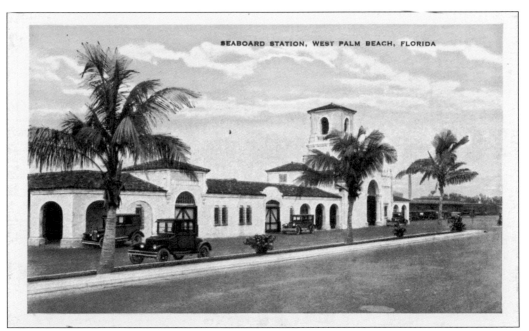

SEABOARD STATION, WEST PALM BEACH, FLORIDA

Harvey and Clarke created this masterpiece for their home city of West Palm Beach at Datura Street and Tamarind Avenue. Built in 1925, it contained elements of the Spanish baroque style with superb ornamentation. Inside there was a palatial fireplace.

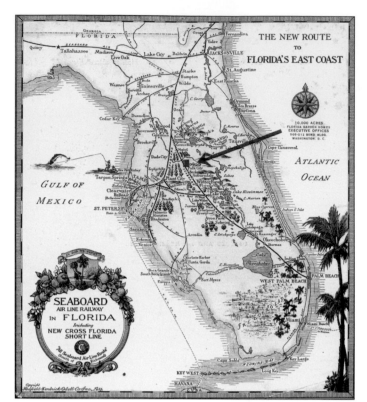

Clearly evident in this 1926 map is the new Seaboard line from Coleman to West Palm Beach. A Washington, D.C., real estate firm—Florida Garden Homes—had 10,000 acres for sale near Polk City, which was pinpointed on the map. Also visible is the new Valrico Cutoff, which enabled trains from Tampa to access the east coast.

Ads like this confirmed that the new Seaboard line to West Palm Beach was open for business. Clarence Barron, publisher of the *Wall Street Journal*, praised Warfield and frequently gave the Seaboard free press.

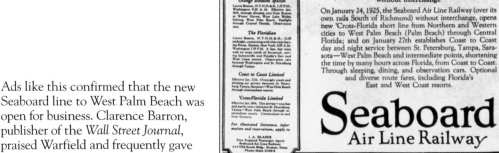

INAUGURATION OF THE

First Through Train Service
to East Coast of Florida
without interchange

On January 24, 1925, the Seaboard Air Line Railway (over its own rails South of Richmond) without interchange, opens new 'Cross-Florida short line from Northern and Western cities to West Palm Beach (Palm Beach) through Central Florida; and on January 27th establishes Coast to Coast day and night service between St. Petersburg, Tampa, Sarasota—West Palm Beach and intermediate points, shortening the time by many hours across Florida, from Coast to Coast. Through sleeping, dining, and observation cars. Optional and diverse route fares, including Florida's East and West Coast resorts.

Seaboard
Air Line Railway

Most every 1920s Seaboard project in Florida was funded through the sale of bonds. The Seaboard All-Florida Railway (a Seaboard subsidiary) built two extensions: West Palm Beach to Miami and another to Fort Myers and Naples. This bond paid six-percent interest.

Groundbreaking for the Seaboard's extension to Miami was held in Hialeah in January 1926. Seaboard president Warfield (center) and Gov. John Martin have their shovels raised for the photographer. (Courtesy Historical Museum of Southern Florida.)

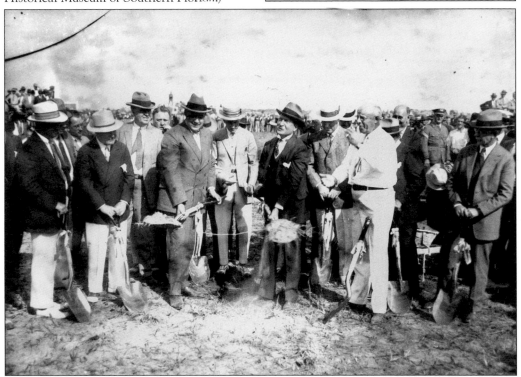

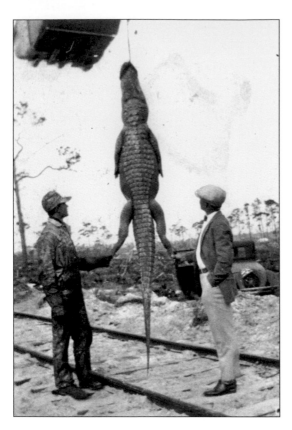

The terrain on both Seaboard All-Florida Railway extensions was not forbidding, though the contractor—Foley Brothers—had to overcome many swamplands. Near Fort Myers, a 12-foot alligator challenged Foley's laborers and lost.

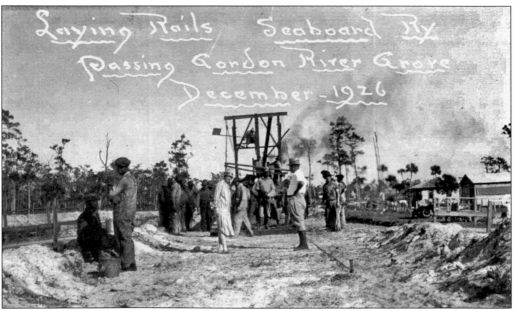

Laying Rails Seaboard Ry Passing Gordon River Grove December - 1926

This wonderful scene was snapped at Gordon River Grove in Naples in December 1926. The contractor's track-laying machine is in the center background. One can almost reach out and touch the stake line. At the far left, two laborers ladle water from a tin can.

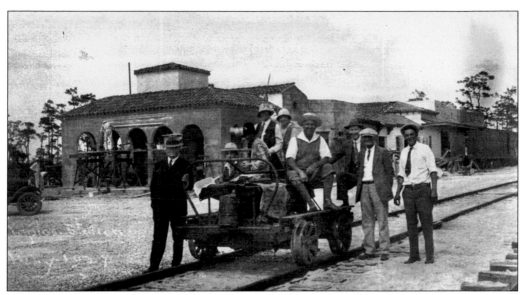

Employees of the Naples Company pose in front of the Seaboard depot in Naples. Harvey and Clarke designed the structure and the one at Fort Myers. Today the Naples structure houses a community center and museum. It was completed in 1928.

Warfield opened the extensions to Naples and Miami in grand style beginning on January 7, 1927. Five separate sections of the *Orange Blossom Special* passenger train accommodated guests, and each invitee received this special commemorative booklet.

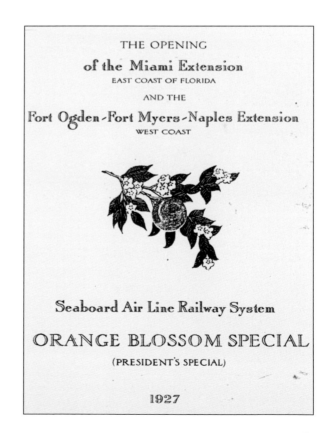

THE OPENING

of the Miami Extension

EAST COAST OF FLORIDA

AND THE

Fort Ogden - Fort Myers - Naples Extension

WEST COAST

Seaboard Air Line Railway System

ORANGE BLOSSOM SPECIAL

(PRESIDENT'S SPECIAL)

1927

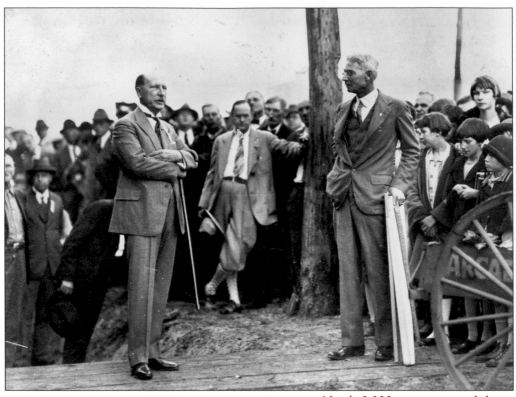

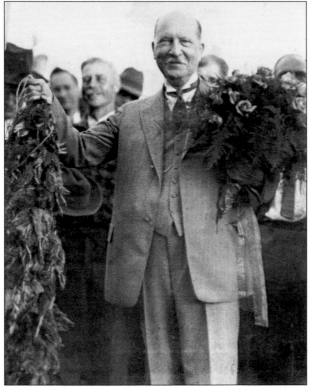

Nearly 2,000 persons greeted the Warfield entourage at Arcadia. Local dignitaries made speeches, as did Gov. John Martin. Kids got the school day off. Warfield appears at left holding a "good luck" cane that he received that morning.

Warfield received bouquets at Arcadia along with 380 quail for the *Blossom* dining cars, which he shows the camera. Tables were set up at the reception, and upon them were locally grown examples of vegetables and citrus.

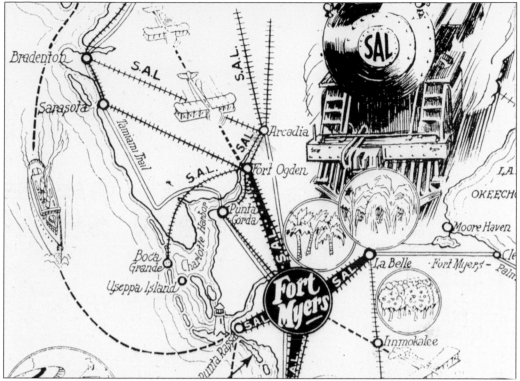

For years, Fort Myers had been ably served by the Atlantic Coast Line Railroad. News of the approaching Seaboard caused a lot of excitement in 1926. This illustration appeared in a local newspaper.

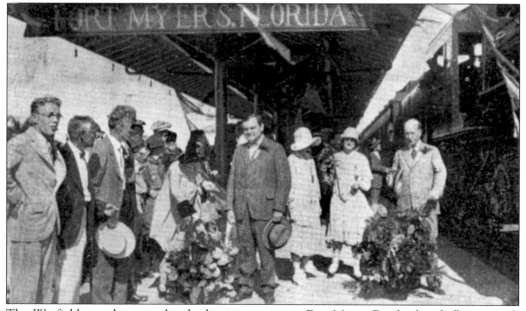

The Warfield crowd was tendered a huge reception at Fort Myers. Bands played, flags waved, and crowds cheered. Then car owners toured *Blossom* guests around the city. Warfield appears on the station platform at far right. Governor Martin is in the center.

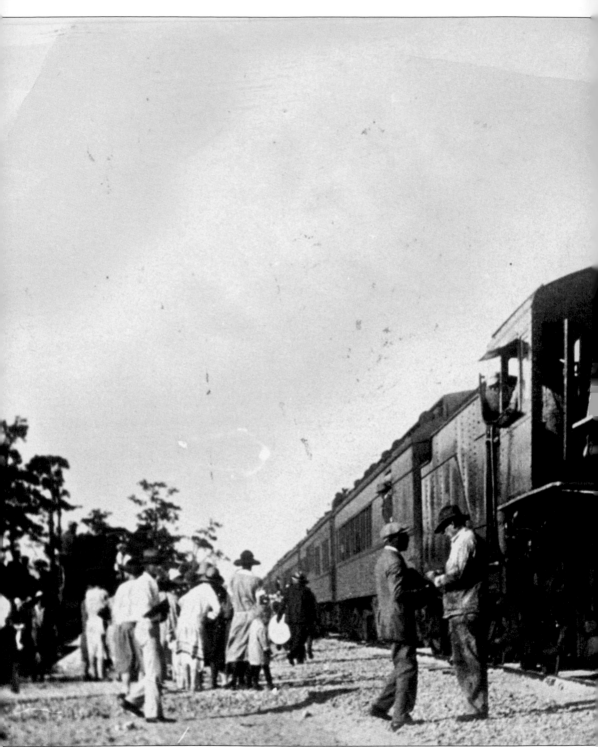

In this wonderful image composed by Robert Fohl Sr., the lead *Orange Blossom Special* section stands proudly at Naples, the train's name prominently displayed below the locomotive headlight. The engineer, whose coveralls are inundated with coal dust, has descended the cab

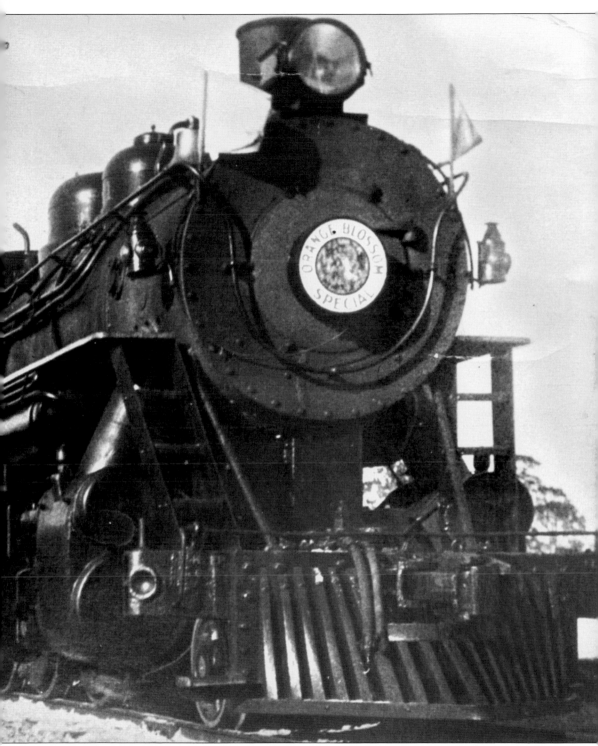

and is speaking with another Seaboard employee. Passengers mingle in the background. No turntable existed at Naples, so later that day, all five *Blossom* sections had to "back up" in convoy style to Fort Myers. Imagine! (Courtesy Railway and Locomotive Historical Society.)

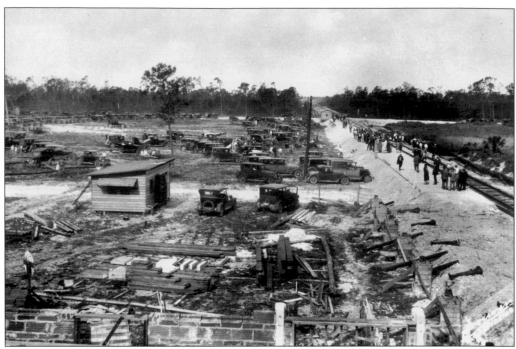

After touring the new "West Coast" extension, the Warfield entourage inspected the one on the east coast. Again huge receptions were staged at station stops, and here the crowds begin to gather at Fort Lauderdale. (Courtesy Historical Museum of Southern Florida.)

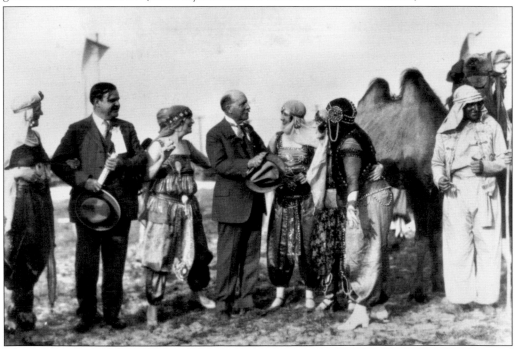

The reception at Opa-Locka was a most unique affair. After words of welcome, locals staged an Arabian scene complete with camels. Here Warfield (center) and Governor Martin (second from left) talk with many of the theatrics. (Courtesy Historical Museum of Southern Florida.)

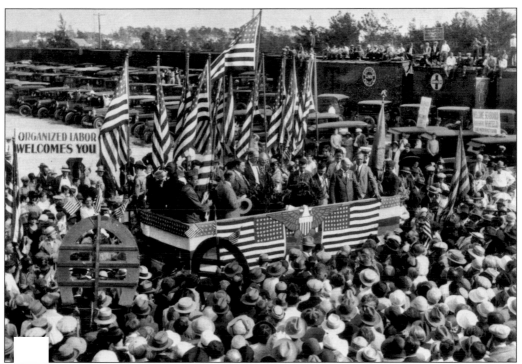

Several thousand greeted the *Blossom* sections at Hialeah. Warfield addressed the multitudes, as did Governor Martin. Upon the platform were several full-blooded Seminole Indians. (Courtesy Historical Museum of Southern Florida.)

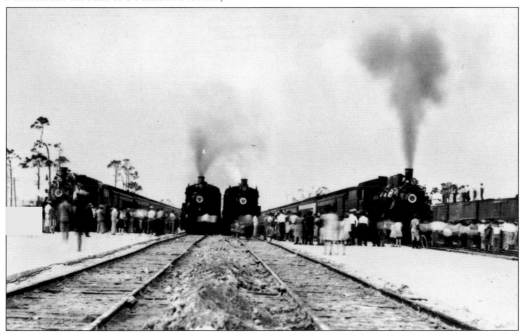

Four sections of the *Orange Blossom Special* can be seen here in the Hialeah yard. Later in the day, all five descended to the Miami station at Seventh Avenue, where the festivities continued. (Courtesy Historical Museum of Southern Florida.)

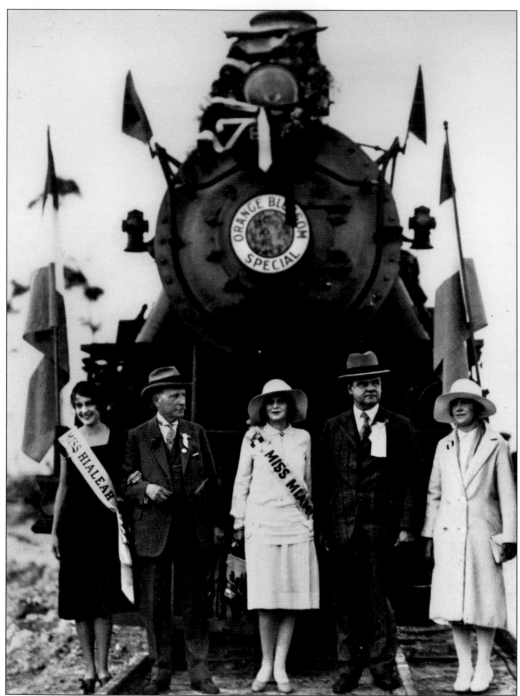

The reigning beauty queens of Hialeah and Miami pose with Warfield (left) and Gov. John Martin. (The governor's wife stands at the far right.) When the *Blossom* trains reached Miami, passengers detrained and were chauffeured by car to Royal Palm Park, where Warfield addressed 5,000 persons. The two-day celebration then came to a close. (Courtesy Historical Museum of Southern Florida.)

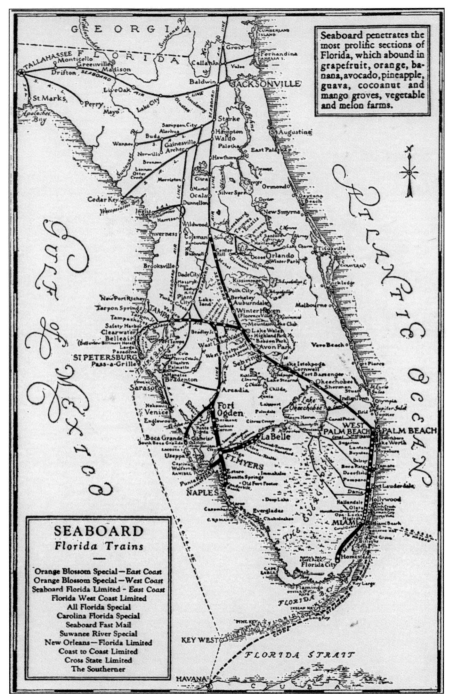

The above map was appended to the aforementioned commemorative booklet. The thick black lines delineate the Seaboard lines recently opened, such as the Gross-Callahan Cutoff, the Valrico Cutoff (Valrico to West Lake Wales), the line from Coleman to West Palm Beach, and the two newest extensions: West Palm Beach to Miami and Florida City, and from Hull (Fort Ogden) down to Fort Myers and Naples with branches to LaBelle and Punta Rassa. That which was built on the west coast was completely torn up by 1953.

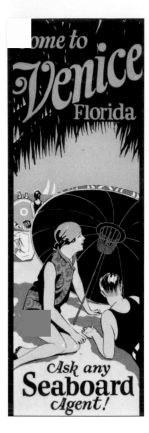

The "city" of Venice, Florida, was created during the boom by America's largest and oldest union—the Brotherhood of Locomotive Engineers. Naturally inviting booklets describing the splendid setting were prepared by the Seaboard.

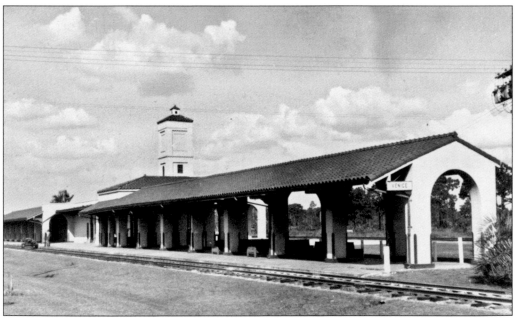

Renowned city planner John Nolen of Boston insisted that an appropriate station be erected at Venice. The Brotherhood of Locomotive Engineers obliged and funded the above structure, which today is magnificently restored.

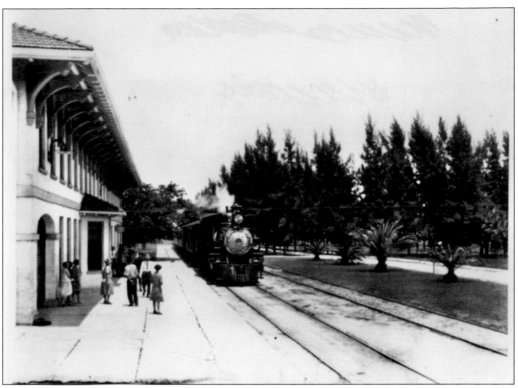

This idyllic scene at Boca Grande was snapped by Burgert Brothers in 1926. A Seaboard train eases into the station, which still stands and is commercially occupied.

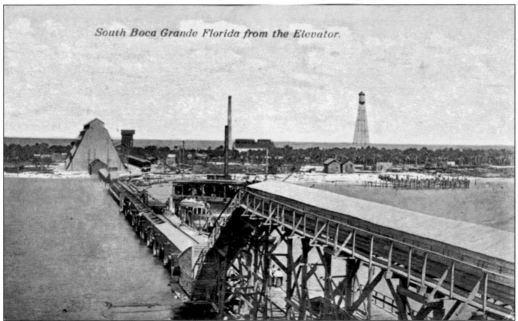

South Boca Grande Florida from the Elevator.

The Seaboard purchased the Charlotte Harbor & Northern during the boom and thus accessed that company's huge phosphate dock at South Boca Grande. Today nothing remains. The former rail route on Gasparilla Island is now a popular bike path.

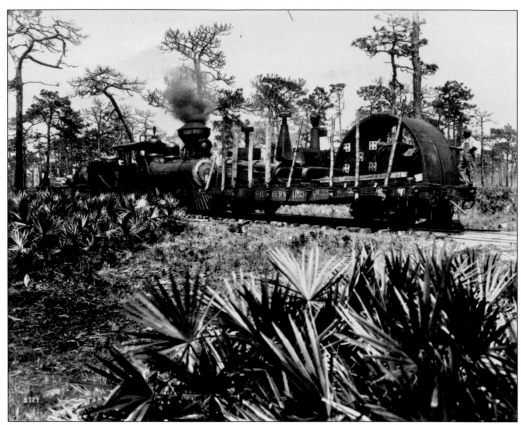

In this 1927 image by Burgert Brothers, a wood-burning locomotive of the Manasota Land and Timber Company is pushing a flat car loaded with mill implements. Its track connected with the Seaboard at Venice. (Courtesy Tampa–Hillsborough County Public Library.)

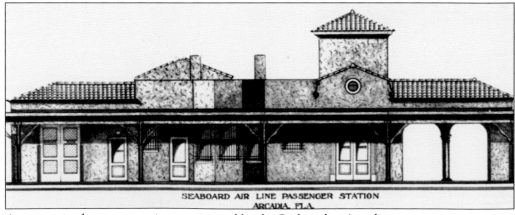

SEABOARD AIR LINE PASSENGER STATION
ARCADIA, FLA.

An attractive boom-era station was erected by the Seaboard at Arcadia, an important junction point where the Seaboard maintained company shops.

Occasionally the Seaboard would extract a testimonial from some famous dignitary, in this case inventor Thomas Edison, who wintered in Fort Myers. The endorsements were woven into ads.

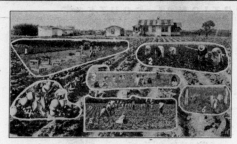

A wide variety of vegetable and fruit crops increases the possibilities for profitable winter farming in Florida. The illustrations show:

- (1) Harvesting celery.
- (2) Picking bell peppers.
- (3) Hired colored labor picking strawberries in December.
- (4) Citrus fruits.
- (5) Harvesting lettuce.
- (6) Gathering snap beans.

A small truck farm home is shown in background.

Thomas A. Edison Says Unlimited Field For Farmers In South

IN A recent interview at his famous winter home at Fort Myers, Florida, Mr. Edison said: "There is an unlimited field for the farmer in the South . . On my field trips through South Florida, I have noticed men clearing land and preparing it for fall. That is working in the right direction." Evidently this noted genius quickly recognized the advantages of Florida, for he has maintained his winter residence there for many years. In fact, it is claimed he lighted his first incandescent light in his experimental work shop at Fort Myers.

TARIFF ON IMPORTED VEGETABLES SHOULD BENEFIT FLORIDA TRUCK FARMERS

Mr. Arthur M. Hyde, Secretary of the U. S. Department of Agriculture, in a recent radio talk stated that the new tariffs will affect approximately $620,000,000 worth of imported agricultural products in both raw and processed forms, based on quantities imported in 1928. Some of the leading commodities that have heretofore been heavily imported are grapefruit, tomatoes, peppers, green peas, string beans, egg-plant, cucumbers and cabbage. Thousands of acres of these and other vegetables and fruits are produced in Florida each year; and there are many locations in that state where climatic and soil conditions combine to offer unsurpassed opportunities for the expansion of these activities to meet the entire demand of the Northern markets in winter.

This Department is in position to assist in the selection of lands and locations suited to practically any phase of agriculture. We have contacts with those who own large and small tracts of desirable farm lands that may be leased by the season, or purchased on terms. Complete data describing opportunities and conditions in specific localities in various districts of Florida, and other states of the Southeast, will be gladly furnished upon request.

"Wealth and fertility unlimited are in Florida soil."—Arthur Brisbane.

SEABOARD AIR LINE RAILWAY

J. N. McBRIDE,

General Agricultural and Land Settlement Agent,
202 Liberty Bank Building, Savannah, Ga.

In Memoriam

RESOLUTIONS OF THE BOARD OF DIRECTORS OF

SEABOARD AIR LINE RAILWAY COMPANY

ADOPTED NOVEMBER 17, 1927,
ON THE DEATH OF

MR. S. DAVIES WARFIELD

CHAIRMAN OF THE BOARD AND PRESIDENT OF THE COMPANY

Resolved, that it is with deep and most sincere regret that the Board of Directors of the Seaboard Air Line Railway Company records the death of Mr. S. Davies Warfield, its distinguished and esteemed Chairman and President of the Company, to whose foresight, fortitude, genius and untiring efforts the present position of the Company as a great and successful railroad system is mainly due.

Railroads, business interests, and owners of railroad securities have on numerous occasions acknowledged their debt of gratitude to Mr. Warfield for having conceived and brought into being the organization of the "National Association of Owners of Railroad Securities," representing and protecting the interests of upwards of $20,000,000,000 of railroad securities, and for having originated and been largely responsible for the enactment of those provisions of the Federal Transportation Act of 1920 which effected a standard for the stabilization of railroad rates to provide for a fair return on the value of property devoted to railroad transportation, thereby not only protecting capital invested in railroad securities but enabling the railroads to obtain necessary capital to keep abreast of the ever growing demands for additional railroad facilities.

Mr. Warfield held the confidence of the owners of securities of the Seaboard Air Line Railway Company, and enjoyed to a most unusual extent the confidence, respect and affection of the officers and employees of the Company whose whole-hearted cooperation was at all times an inspiration and a source of real pleasure to him.

Unspoiled by numerous testimonials of the esteem and regard in which he was held by the people and public officials of the territory served by the Seaboard Air Line Railway, he created a most enviable position and good will for the Company, the preservation of which will be sacredly guarded by those who are to carry on his work.

It is to be sincerely regretted that Mr. Warfield did not live to see his plans for the complete development of the Railway, and all his hopes and aspirations, realized in full, but the spirit instilled by him in the Seaboard organization will carry on until the goal of his unselfish ambition for the Company is reached.

In our knowledge and appreciation of the success of Mr. Warfield's efforts on behalf of the Seaboard Air Line Railway Company, we are not unmindful of his accomplishments in other business activities, as well as in public life, in both of which he won well-deserved recognition for ability, character and honesty of purpose.

To have known Mr. Warfield, as we have been privileged to know him, has been an inspiration for the attainment of the higher and loftier things of life, of which no better evidence is possible than the disposition by his will, of substantially all the material results of his strenuous life's work, in memory of his mother, for the alleviation of the sufferings and unhappiness of dependent aged women.

In life Mr. Warfield was a man distinguished and esteemed among men, and in departing he left a record of accomplishment which will be a constant inspiration to those to whom is now entrusted the fulfillment of his high hopes and aspirations.

To Mr. Warfield's relatives the Board of Directors extends its most sincere sympathy.

Further Resolved, that a copy of these resolutions be engrossed and presented to the Anna Emory Warfield Home for Aged Women upon its organization, to be preserved as a testimonial of the regard and affection of the Board of Directors of the Seaboard Air Line Railway Company for its late Chairman.

Warfield died just as the Seaboard was beginning to experience financial difficulties. The boom in Florida was over, and the cost of servicing all that Seaboard debt was taking a toll. Warfield's millions were left to charity.

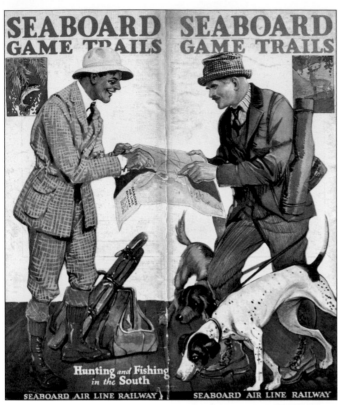

SEABOARD GAME TRAILS   SEABOARD GAME TRAILS

Hunting *and* Fishing
in the South

SEABOARD AIR LINE RAILWAY   SEABOARD AIR LINE RAILWAY

The Seaboard always sought passenger traffic, and far be it from the company not to solicit sportsmen. To entice them to the territory served, the railway prepared this guidebook in 1922. It was geared to fisher folk and hunters.

The *Orange Blossom Special* was the Seaboard's flagship passenger train. Service to Miami and St. Petersburg was furnished (and to other points) as this 1928 timetable confirms. Woe unto any employee or train that delayed the *Blossom's* flight!

FLORIDA'S DISTINGUISHED WINTER TRAIN

ORANGE BLOSSOM SPECIAL

All Pullman De Luxe   One Night Out   No Extra Fare

NEW YORK and WASHINGTON to FLORIDA

TO THE EAST COAST—THE WEST COAST

THROUGH THE SCENIC HIGHLAND AND LAKE SECTION OF CENTRAL FLORIDA BY DAYLIGHT

Connection with Clyde Line Steamships to and from Havana   Connections to and from Palmetto-Bradenton-Sarasota-Venice and Fort Myers

CLUB—LIBRARY CAR—BARBER, VALET, BATH—OBSERVATION LIBRARY
CAR—LADIES' LOUNGE, BATH, MAID - MANICURIST — DINING CARS.

Coaches on the West Coast "Orange Blossom Special"—Between Jacksonville and St. Petersburg.

FOR EXPLANATION OF CHARACTERS SOUTHBOUND, SEE PAGE 10. NORTHBOUND, PAGE 14.
FOR CONSIST OF TRAINS SOUTHBOUND, SEE PAGES 15-16. NORTHBOUND, PAGES 17-18.

SEABOARD AIR LINE RAILWAY

"Through the Heart of the South"

80

Four

INVASION OF THE FRISCO

Thus far, we have explored what Florida's "Big Three" railroads achieved during the 1920s. However, one important story played out that decade that had no connection to the boom nor the Big Three. It involved a completely new player from the Midwest.

The St. Louis–San Francisco Railway Company ("Frisco") was a big and profitable transportation entity based in St. Louis. The Frisco System operated 5,630 miles of track in Missouri, Kansas, Oklahoma, Arkansas, Texas, Tennessee, Mississippi, and Alabama. The company was formed in the 1870s, several reorganizations later took place, and a new Frisco railway company emerged in 1916.

By 1925, revenues on the Frisco amounted to $94.7 million. Like most American railways, the company made its serious money in the carriage of freight, not moving people, though it certainly operated its share of passenger trains. The Frisco's biggest freight commodity—generating 38 percent of all freight revenues—were the "products of mines" such as coal, coke, iron ore, clay, gravel, stone, petroleum, asphalt, and salt. Agricultural products were the second biggest freight item—wheat, corn, oats, grain, flour, hay, straw, alfalfa, tobacco, cotton, and to a lesser degree citrus, potatoes, and fresh vegetables. The third biggest category was livestock and animal by-products.

Although the Frisco served many river settings, the company lacked a real ocean port, where freight could be off-loaded from railroad cars into awaiting ships and dispatched to the far corners of the globe. This impediment nagged at Pres. James Kurn and the Frisco board, especially after the company obtained an entrance into industrial Birmingham, Alabama. Finding an ocean port connection for its Alabama coal became a pressing need. Fortunately a window of opportunity arose in 1924.

The greatest Florida port on the Gulf of Mexico was at Pensacola, whose deepwater harbor had been coveted by business and the military since the American Civil War. For many decades, the mighty Louisville & Nashville Railroad monopolized the setting, though several small short lines maintained a presence. The L&N erected substantial docks at Pensacola, and from here the company dispatched vast quantities of freight, lumber, and coal. When one of those small carriers in Pensacola became available to purchase, the Frisco swung into action.

The Muscle Shoals, Birmingham & Pensacola Railroad operated between Pensacola and Kimbrough, Alabama, via remote piney forests and sparsely populated towns. The Muscle Shoals entity was really a reincarnation of the Gulf, Florida & Alabama Railroad, a rickety concern that had inadequate traffic, poor finances, and a discouraged management. The GF&A was sold at foreclosure in 1922 to Robert Fischer who, in turn, deeded it to the Muscle Shoals entity. In December 1925, the Frisco purchased the line for $305,000. Included in the sale was the company's valuable dock at the Pensacola waterfront, which was a stone's throw away from those owned by the L&N.

After obtaining the Muscle Shoals firm, two fresh challenges faced the Frisco board; getting the Muscle Shoals route into shape for trunk line traffic and building a physical connection between Kimbrough and the Frisco system. Frisco engineers immediately tackled the challenges and prepared cost estimates. The most cost-effective solution for uniting the two concerns was to build a short-cut between Kimbrough and Aberdeen, Mississippi, by way of Demopolis, Alabama. According to the Frisco's 1926 annual report, the 152-mile connection became "the corporation's most important project planned for 1926 and 1927." President Kurn predicted that 90-car freight trains would eventually pass over the line, carrying oil and wheat originating in Kansas and Oklahoma, along with manufactured goods produced in Kansas City and St. Louis. Contracts were let in early 1926.

The Frisco also spent $2.5 million on modernizing the Muscle Shoals line out of Pensacola. Excessive grades were eliminated, cuts were widened, thousands of new cross ties were installed, new steel rail was laid, all lightly constructed bridges and trestles were replaced, new water towers were built, and every platform, freight house, and station along the route was renewed. Additionally the terminal facilities at Pensacola were enlarged.

The Frisco opened its new route to Pensacola on June 27, 1928, using two special passenger trains. On board the *Pensacola Special* was President Kurn and board chairman E. N. Brown along with 300 businessmen, bankers, and railway officers from the Midwest. Pensacola itself declared a city holiday, storefronts were gaily decorated, and festivities included a parade, banquet, and a regatta on Escambia Bay. Regular passenger train service from St. Louis and Kansas City to Pensacola commenced in early September. And in this way, a big and prosperous Midwestern carrier figured into Florida railroad history.

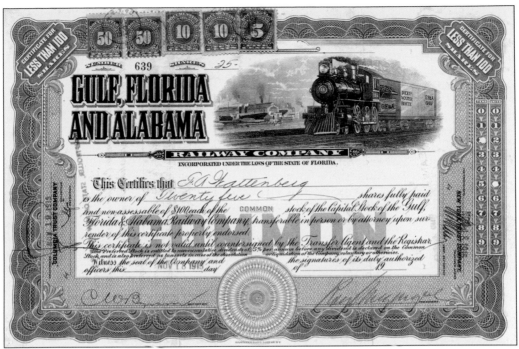

The Gulf, Florida & Alabama Railroad is largely erased from the public's memory. It operated from Pensacola to Kimbrough, Alabama, through piney woodlands and sparse communities. But it did have one saving grace: a splendid dock on Pensacola harbor.

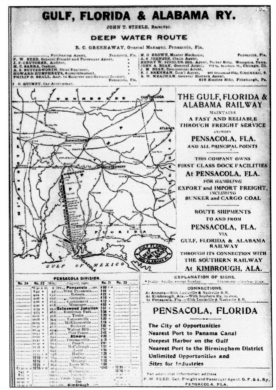

Despite its important dock at Pensacola, the financial condition of the GF&A was rickety. It also had weak management and a very little traffic. When this 1920 advertisement appeared, the company was in the hands of receivers.

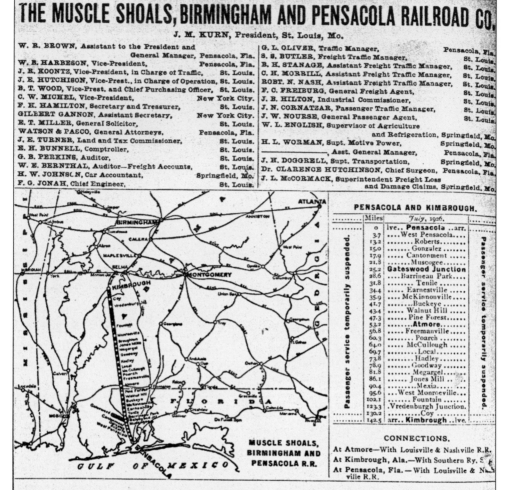
The Muscle Shoals, Birmingham & Pensacola Railroad was a reincarnation of the GF&A. Despite its new name and owners, business remained sluggish. When this advertisement appeared in 1926, the company was owned by yet another party—the Frisco.

Connecting the Muscle Shoals road with the Frisco System required a new line between Kimbrough, Alabama, and Aberdeen, Mississippi. When completed, commodities produced in Midwestern states could be channeled to the Frisco's new Gulf port at Pensacola. In conjunction with the new cutoff (see broken line on map), the Muscle Shoals route from Kimbrough to Pensacola was modernized for $2.5 million.

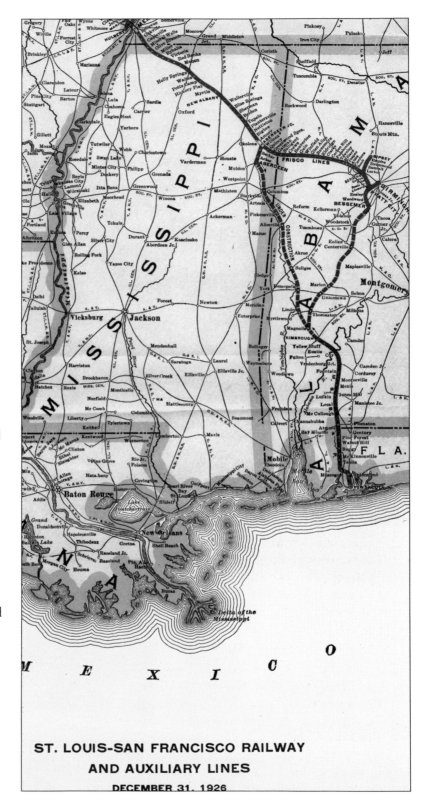

ST. LOUIS-SAN FRANCISCO RAILWAY
AND AUXILIARY LINES
DECEMBER 31, 1926

The city of Pensacola went out of its way to accommodate the Frisco, for it meant the Louisville & Nashville Railroad's monopoly on the Gulf port would be broken. It has not been learned what the L&N thought of the Frisco invasion.

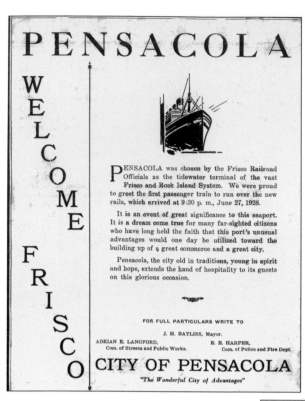

PENSACOLA

WELCOME FRISCO

PENSACOLA was chosen by the Frisco Railroad Officials as the tidewater terminal of the vast Frisco and Rock Island System. We were proud to greet the first passenger train to run over the new rails, which arrived at 9:30 p. m., June 27, 1928.

It is an event of great significance to this seaport. It is a dream come true for many far-sighted citizens who have long held the faith that this port's unusual advantages would one day be utilized toward the building up of a great commerce and a great city.

Pensacola, the city old in traditions, young in spirit and hope, extends the hand of hospitality to its guests on this glorious occasion.

FOR FULL PARTICULARS WRITE TO

J. H. BAYLISS, Mayor.

ADRIAN E. LANGFORD,
Com. of Streets and Public Works.

E. E. HARPER,
Com. of Police and Fire Dept.

CITY OF PENSACOLA

"The Wonderful City of Advantages"

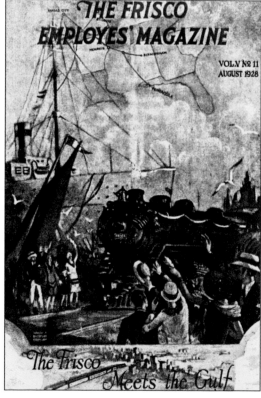

This edition of the Frisco employees' magazine paid tribute to the new route to Pensacola. Several articles described the Muscle Shoals modernization and how the line was built from Kimbrough to Aberdeen.

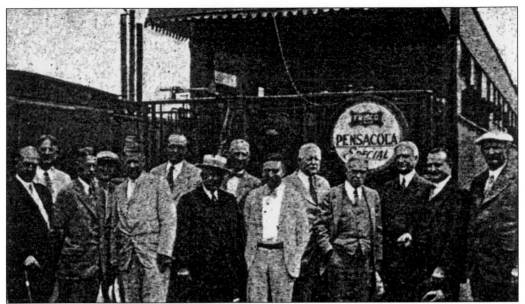

To open its new terminal on the Gulf, Frisco officials and guests came to Pensacola on two sections of the *Pensacola Special*. The city staged an impressive welcome. Five thousand people witnessed the parade and air show, and every storefront was decorated.

The Frisco's arrival inspired Messrs. Ruben and Runyan to compose a song. Soon every pianist in Pensacola wanted a copy.

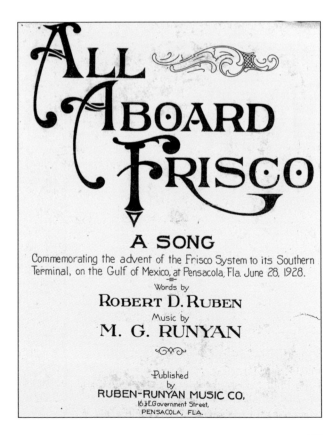

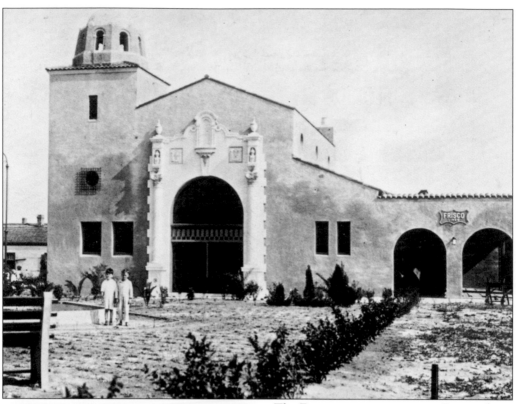

The Frisco passenger station in Pensacola, which fronted Garden Street, was built in the Spanish Mission style. Sadly it was demolished in 1967.

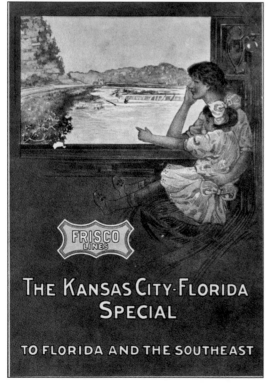

FRISCO
LINES

THE KANSAS CITY-FLORIDA
SPECIAL

TO FLORIDA AND THE SOUTHEAST

Interestingly the Frisco offered train service to Florida long before its 1928 debut at Pensacola. *The Kansas City-Florida Special* ran between Kansas City and Jacksonville by way of Memphis, in conjunction with other railroad companies.

Five

HERE AND THERE

During the fabled 1920s, the Big Three—the Florida East Coast, Seaboard Air Line, and Atlantic Coast Line—owned about 85 percent of all rail mileage within Florida. The ACL possessed the most, the Seaboard came in second, and the FEC was a distant third. There were also many smaller players, most of which did not profit from boom fever per se.

The next biggest player size-wise was the Louisville & Nashville Railroad, which operated 245 miles of track in the Sunshine State. Its route descended into Pensacola from Flomaton, Alabama, whereupon it headed across the Panhandle to River Junction by way of Crestview. The company operated several branches (see map) and a clutch of firms depended on the L&N for a connection to the outside world.

It was through a subsidiary (the Georgia, Southern & Florida) that the mighty Southern Railway maintained a presence in Florida. Two branches emanated from Valdosta, Georgia: one to Jacksonville by way of Crawford, while another wended its way to Palatka via Lake City and Lake Butler. In all, the Southern Railway operated about 150 miles of track within the Sunshine State.

Based in Port St. Joe, the 96-mile Apalachicola Northern Railroad reached northwards to River Junction. During the 1920s, the company also operated a small terminal railway at Port St. Joe together with a land company and an inn.

The Atlanta & St. Andrews Bay Railway was headquartered in Panama City. The company owned nearly eight-five miles of track between Panama City and Dothan, Alabama, by way of Cottondale. During the 1920s, Panama City experienced an uptick in real estate activities, but transactions did not reach a frenzied pitch.

When it came to the transportation of logs and lumber products, Florida's Live Oak, Perry & Gulf Railroad was in a class of its own. The mills it served furnished a good deal of lumber for boom projects elsewhere in the state. It also operated several passenger trains, though the movement of freight generated its major revenues.

The Frisco Railway, whose story was taken up in chapter four, operated a mere 47 miles of track within Florida.

This brings us to the 45-mile Marianna & Blountstown, which operated between those two Florida communities. (At Marianna, a connection was made with the aforementioned L&N Railroad.) Smaller yet was the Tavares & Gulf Railroad and the Jacksonville, Gainesville & Gulf, both of which were leased to the Seaboard in the 1920s. The remaining bit players included the South Georgia Railway (Adel, Georgia, to Hampton Springs, Florida), the Alabama & Western Florida, the St. Johns River Terminal Company, the Jacksonville Terminal Railroad, the Georgia & Florida, and the 10-mile Trans Florida Central between Sebastian and Fellsmere, which depended on the Florida East Coast Railway for outside connections.

The Big Three operated many famous passenger trains to and within Florida during the boom. In fact, several out-of-state companies also vied for the long-distance traffic, especially to such Midwest points as Chicago, Detroit, Cincinnati, Kansas City, and St. Louis. To attract customers, each company issued fancy brochures and pamphlets, which described a particular train at length along with the route taken.

One line to Florida from the Midwest that enjoyed a very large clientele during the boom was the famous Dixie Route. At the boom's height, three separate Dixie Route trains were operated to the Sunshine State: the *Dixie Flyer*, the *Dixie Express*, and the *Dixie Limited*. Another popular 1920s train was the elegant *Royal Palm*. The big and powerful Illinois Central Railroad dispatched two famous consists to Florida—*The Seminole* and *The Floridan*. And on went the list. It might be noted that the first through train from New York to Florida—the *Florida Special*—was operated by the Atlantic Coast Line Railroad on January 9, 1887. The service was sponsored by car builder George Pullman, who financed the train's construction. It covered the 1,074-mile trip in 31 hours and ran on a tri-weekly basis. By 1928, some 32 trains were operating between New York and Florida via the ACL and Seaboard Railroads.

In the pages ahead, we present some representative timetables and literature of the 1920s, and hasten to ask: would the modern generation avail themselves of these wonderful trains and services if they were offered today?

The Louisville & Nashville Railroad was the fourth-largest railroad that served Florida. For years, it ably served Pensacola and the Panhandle. Unfortunately the land boom only made a slight impression upon this part of the Sunshine State.

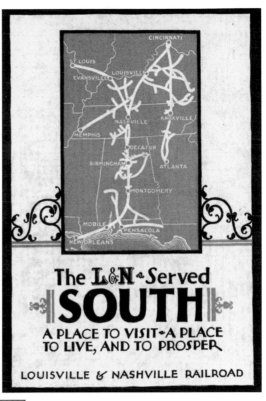

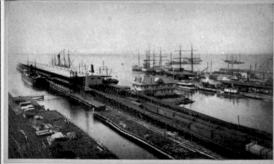

A VIEW OF PENSACOLA HARBOR

THE PRINCIPAL industry in *West Florida*, the one employing more men and representing the investment of more money, is the cutting and marketing of *Lumber*—some of the greatest mills in the entire South being located west of the Apalachicola River and converting great logs of *Pine*, *Cypress* and other Southern woods into planks and dressed lumber for distribution throughout the entire United States. A great deal of this timber is exported through the port of Pensacola and the industry gives employment to several thousand people.

With the cutting out of the forests and the steadily increasing population in *West Florida*, lands are being cleared for both *Farm* and *Factory-site* purposes and all kinds of *Commercial Industries* are being started and developed—*Packing Plants* for *Live Stock*, *Fruits* and *Vegetable Products* and for *Sea-Foods* of all kinds.

With the introduction of cheap *Hydro-Electric Power* into the Gulf Coast section of *West Florida*, the manufacturer, seeking a location where *Labor* is cheap and plentiful, where *Power* is cheap and adequate (45,000 horsepower hydro-electric current service now available), can do no better than to consider this land of mild temperatures, good roads, good schools and good living conditions, where he is near to the sources of supply of practically every raw material used in American industries.

There are many attractive business propositions in West Florida, about which this Railroad will be glad to give full data. Understand, of course, this Railroad cannot undertake to secure employment for readers of this booklet, but, without charge, it will lend its every effort to give full and authoritative advice on the industrial possibilities in West Florida.

Several major docks comprised the Pensacola terminal of the L&N Railroad. Vast quantities of coal, lumber products, and other commodities were dispatched from here to destinations around the globe.

91

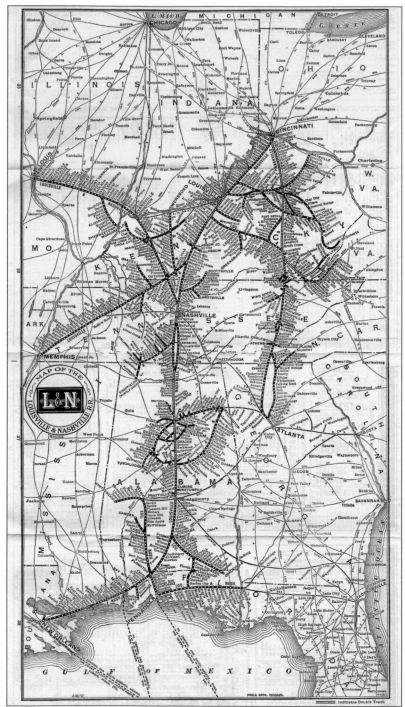

This map reveals how extensive the L&N System in mid-America really was. Its route into Florida descended to Pensacola from Flomaton, Alabama, whereupon it went east across the Panhandle to River Junction by way of Crestview. The company operated several branches, notably between Crestview and Duval, Alabama, and into Graceville. Further a few companies depended on the L&N to reach the outside world.

92

In addition to running local passenger service, the L&N jointly operated several prominent Midwestern trains to the Sunshine State, as this 1928 timetable confirms.

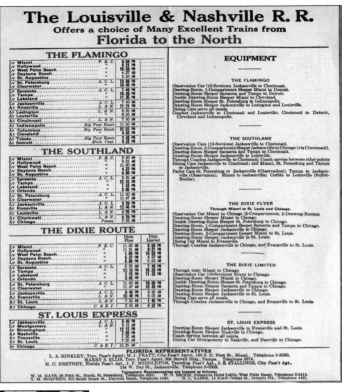

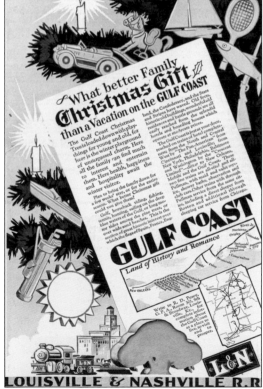

During the 1920s, the L&N ran a series of interesting advertisements. This one played up an unusual Christmas gift for the family: a Gulf coast vacation.

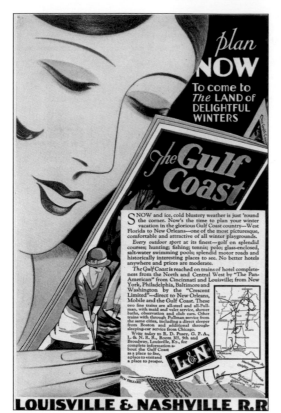

A flapper studies the possibilities of the Gulf Coast in this 1926 advertisement. Just how many passengers it drew to the West Florida–New Orleans territory of the L&N is not known.

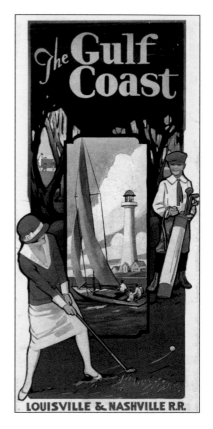

A popular L&N booklet of the 1920s was entitled "The Gulf Coast." It contained a list of attractions and places to stay, together with inviting photographs. The cover, like so many of the era, featured pastel colors.

This description of Florida appeared in the 1927 issue of "The Gulf Coast." Every city served by the L&N was mentioned. As always, the trick was to get winter-weary tourists and vacationers to the Sunshine State, hopefully by way of L&N trains.

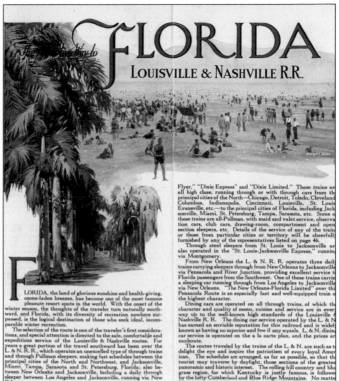

FLORIDA, the land of glorious sunshine and health-giving. ozone-laden breezes, has become one of the most famous pleasure resort spots in the world. With the onset of the winter season, the thoughts of the traveler turn naturally southward, and Florida, with its diversity of recreation nowhere surpassed, is the logical destination of those who seek ideal, incomparable winter recreation.

The selection of the route is one of the traveler's first considerations, and special attention is directed to the safe, comfortable and expeditious service of the Louisville & Nashville routes. For years a great portion of the travel southward has been over the L. & N. R. R., which operates an unexcelled type of through trains and through Pullman sleepers, making fast schedules between the principal cities of the North and Northwest, and Jacksonville, Miami, Tampa, Sarasota and St. Petersburg, Florida; also between New Orleans and Jacksonville, including a daily through sleeper between Los Angeles and Jacksonville, running via New Orleans.

The five principal through Florida trains via this railroad from the North are known for their exceptional service, safety and time. They are named "The Flamingo," "The Southland," "Dixie Flyer," "Dixie Express" and "Dixie Limited." These trains are all high class, running through or with through cars from the principal cities of the North—Chicago, Detroit, Toledo, Cleveland, Columbus, Indianapolis, Cincinnati, Louisville, St. Louis, Evansville, etc.—to the principal cities of Florida, including Jacksonville, Miami, St. Petersburg, Tampa, Sarasota, etc. Some of these trains are all-Pullman, with maid and valet service, observation cars, club cars, drawing-room, compartment and open section sleepers, etc. Details of the service of any of the trains or those from particular cities or territory will be cheerfully furnished by any of the representatives listed on page 46.

Through steel sleepers from St. Louis to Jacksonville are also operated in the "St. Louis-Jacksonville Express," running via Montgomery.

From New Orleans the L. & N. R. R. operates three daily trains carrying sleepers through from New Orleans to Jacksonville via Pensacola and River Junction, providing excellent service to Florida passengers from the Southwest. One of these trains carries a sleeping car running through from Los Angeles to Jacksonville via New Orleans. "The New Orleans-Florida Limited" over this Pensacola Route is an especially fast and well-equipped train of the highest character.

Dining cars are operated on all through trains, of which the character and quality of menu, cuisine and service are in every way up to the well-known high standards of the Louisville & Nashville R. R. The dining car service operated by the L. & N. has earned an enviable reputation for this railroad and is widely known as having no superior and few if any equals. L. & N. dining car service is operated on the a la carte plan, and the prices are moderate.

The routes traveled by the trains of the L. & N. are such as to delight the eye and inspire the patriotism of every loyal American. The schedules are arranged, as far as possible, so that the tourist may traverse by daylight, those sections of the greatest panoramic and historic interest. The rolling hill country and blue grass region, for which Kentucky is justly famous, is followed by the lofty Cumberland and Blue Ridge Mountains. No matter how many mountain ranges the traveler has seen, the Appalachian Range, with its great forested slopes, softly picturesque, has a distinctive beauty which is unique as well as inspiring.

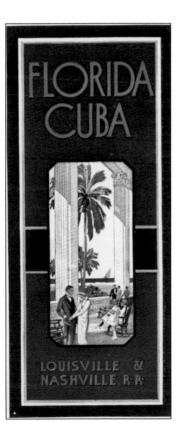

Many Midwestern tourists enjoyed Florida and Cuba. This L&N booklet focused on both destinations and in particular what the traveler could expect to see in continental Havana.

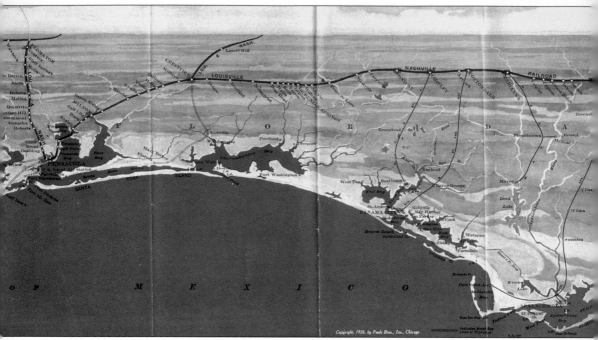

As this artist's map of the 1920s confirms, the L&N dominated the Panhandle. At River Junction (far upper right), the L&N handed over traffic to the Seaboard Air Line Railway destined for Jacksonville and other points. But that relationship was carefully monitored, for the L&N was owned by the Seaboard's rival, the Atlantic Coast Line Railroad, a purchase that Henry Walters had overseen years before.

THE FLAMINGO

BETWEEN

DETROIT, TOLEDO, CLEVELAND, COLUMBUS, INDIANAPOLIS, CINCINNATI, LOUISVILLE and MIAMI, TAMPA and ST. PETERSBURG

Southbound	STATIONS.	Northbound
12 05 p.m.	lve. DETROIT ....(Michigan Central) arr.	4 23 p.m.
1 45 p.m.	lve. TOLEDO.....................(C. C. C. & St. L.) arr.	2 43 p.m.
12 00 Noon	lve CLEVELAND ....(C. C. C. & St L.) arr.	4 55 p.m.
3 15 p.m.	lve. COLUMBUS .... " arr.	12 55 p.m.
3 20 p.m.	lve. INDIANAPOLIS ....(C. C. C. & St L.) arr.	11 50 a.m.
7 00 p.m.	lve. CINCINNATI ....(Louisville & Nashville) arr.	7 40 a.m.
5 40 p.m.	lve. LOUISVILLE ....(Louisville & Nashville) arr.	8 55 a.m
8 25 p.m.	lve. LEXINGTON .... " arr.	6 05 a.m.
8 20 a.m.	arr. ATLANTA ....(Louisville & Nashville) lve.	6 20 p.m.
11 25 a.m.	arr. MACON.....................(Central of Georgia) lve.	3 15 p.m.
2 30 p.m.	arr. ALBANY .... " lve.	12 10 p.m.
9 00 p.m.	arr. JACKSONVILLE ....(Atlantic Coast Line) lve.	7 40 a.m.
10 00 p.m.	lve. JACKSONVILLE ....(Florida East Coast) arr.	6 50 a.m.
8 00 a.m.	arr. MIAMI .... " lve.	8 50 p.m
10 30 p.m.	lve. JACKSONVILLE ....(Atlantic Coast Line) arr.	6 30 a.m.
6 00 a.m.	arr. TAMPA .... " lve.	10 30 p.m.
8 45 a.m.	arr. SARASOTA .... " lve.	7 40 p.m.
10 30 p.m.	lve. JACKSONVILLE ....(Atlantic Coast Line) arr.	6 30 a.m.
7 45 a.m.	arr. ST. PETERSBURG .... " lve.	10 00 p.m.

EQUIPMENT

Drawing-room, 1 Compt. Sleeping Car between Detroit and Miami.
Drawing-room Sleeping Car between Detroit and Sarasota.
Drawing-room Sleeping Car between Cleveland and Miami.
Drawing-room Sleeping Car between Indianapolis and St. Petersburg.
Drawing-room Sleeping Car between Cincinnati and Atlanta.

Drawing-room Sleeping Car between Louisville, Lexington and Jacksonville.
Observation Car between Cincinnati and Jacksonville.
Dining Car serves all meals.
Through Coaches between Cincinnati and Jacksonville.
Coach service between all points.

THE SOUTHLAND

Between Chicago, Cincinnati, Louisville and Florida

Southbound	STATIONS.	Northbound
9 15 P M	lve. Chicago ....(Pennsylvania) arr.	7 55 A M
6 20 A M	arr. Cincinnati, ... " lve.	11 55 P M
7 10 A M	lve. Cincinnati......(L. & N.).(L. & N.-Penna. Sta.) arr.	9 20 P M
6 40 A M	lve. Louisville ....(Louisville & Nashville) arr.	9 20 P M
3 26 P M	arr. Knoxville ....(Louisville & Nashville) lve.	12 56 P M
8 55 P M	arr. Atlanta	7 25 A M
12 05 A M	arr. Macon ....(Central of Georgia) lve.	4 15 A M
3 20 A M	arr. Albany .... " lve.	12 55 A M
9 50 A M	arr. Jacksonville ....(Atlantic Coast Line) lve.	8 20 P M
10 00 A M	lve. Jacksonville ....(Atlantic Coast Line) arr.	7 35 P M
8 05 P M	arr. Tampa .... " lve.	12 15 P M
....	arr. Sarasota .... " lve.	9 25 A M

EQUIPMENT

Drawing-room, 2-Compartment Sleeper between Chicago and Jacksonville, via Cincinnati.
Drawing-room Sleeper between Cincinnati and Jacksonville.
Drawing-room Sleeper Sarasota and Tampa to Cincinnati (north-

Drawing-room Sleeper between Louisville and Jacksonville (open 9 50 p.m. evening previous to departure).
Observation Car and Dining Car between Cincinnati and Jacksonville.
Buffet Parlor Car between Louisville and Corbin.

Two popular L&N trains to Florida during the boom were *The Flamingo* and *The Southland*. As this 1926 timetable notes, both trains utilized L&N rails for part of the journey.

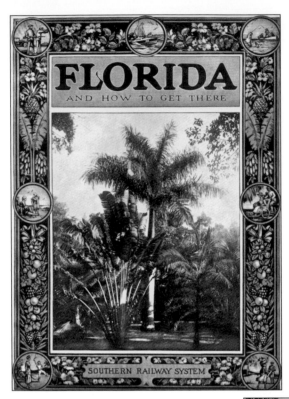

The Southern Railway maintained a small presence in Florida. Nevertheless it produced several publications during the boom. This one, issued in 1923, described the state's recreational pleasures.

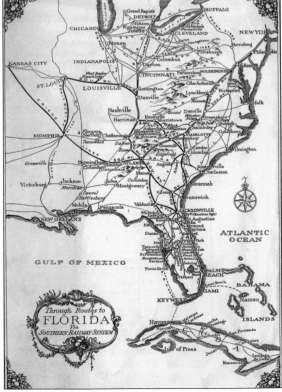

The Southern Railway's mainline ran between Washington, D.C., and Atlanta. At Valdosta, Georgia, the company operated a route into Jacksonville proper via Crawford and another into Palatka by way of Lake City, Lake Butler, and Hampton.

Florida's "Big Three" railroads did an extraordinary business in the 1920s. The state's small players did not prosper as much. Nevertheless the Apalachicola Northern carved out a modest existence.

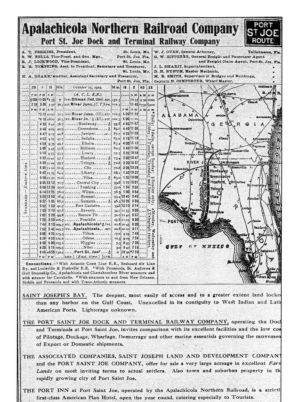

Another small player was the Atlanta & St. Andrews Bay, which operated between Panama City and Dothan, Alabama. Bay County witnessed a small amount of boom fever in the 1920s but nothing like what occurred on the peninsula.

ATLANTA & SAINT ANDREWS BAY RAILWAY
"THE BAY LINE."

MINOR C. KEITH, Prest., New York. ————, Sec'y & Treas., New York.
W. C. SHERMAN, Executive JOHN B. PRUYN, Gen. Counsel,
  Vice-Prest., Panama City, Fla.   New York.
H. W. WOOLF, V.-P. & Gen. Mgr., ✱ Dr. A. S. FRASIER, Cht. Surg., Dothan, Ala.
G. B. WRIGHT, Acting Auditor, ✱ A. M. LEWIS, Mast. Mechanic, Millville, Fla.

	3	1	Ms	November 21, 1926.	2	4	
	P M	A M		LEAVE] [ARRIVE	A M	P M	
	*2 55	*10 50	0	.... Dothan[1]	11 50	5 30	
	3 16	11 08	10	...... Hodgesville	11 28	5 02	
	3 26	11 17	14	...... Madrid	11 19	4 56	
	3 40	11 29	19	...... Campbellton	11 04	4 44	
	4 10	11 55	30	arr ... Cottondale ... lve.	10 34	4 22	
	4 25	11 55	30	lve ... Cottondale[2] .. arr.	10 25	4 15	
	4 42	12 10	37	.... Alford	10 09	3 53	
	4 54	12 18	40	...... Round Lake	10 01	3 51	
	5 05	12 31	45	..... Compass Lake	9 48	3 40	
	5 23	12 49	53	.... Fountain	9 25	3 19	
	5 40	1 05	61	...... Youngstown	9 05	3 02	
	6 24	1 42	80	} .. Millville Junction .. { } .. Lynn Haven Station . {	8 20	2 24	
	6 30	1 50	82	..... Panama City	*8 15	*2 20	
	P M	P M		ARRIVE] [LEAVE	A M	P M	

Trains marked ✱ run daily. STANDARD—Central time.

Connections.—[1] With Central of Georgia Ry. and with Atlantic Coast Line R.R. & Nashville R.R. [2] With Louisville & Nashville R.R.

LIVE OAK, PERRY & GULF RAILROAD.

—, Chairman of Board.
W. T. Hargrett, Prest. and Gen. Mgr.
R. P. Hopkins, Sec'y-Treas. and Traffic Manager.
C. R. Wadsworth, Superintendent.
H. Sivia, Auditor.
John F. Harrell, Gen. Counsel.
J. T. Bohen, Master Mechanic.
G. P. Kellam, Roadmaster.
Dr. H. M. Strickland, Chief Surgeon.
General Offices—Live Oak, Fla.

13	11	3	1	5	Mls.	February 21, 1926. (Eastern time.)	4	6	2	14	12
PM	AM	PM	AM	AM			AM	PM	PM	AM	PM
§2 25	§8 00	†12 15	†7 00	†6 50	0	lve..Live Oak¹ ᵟ arr.	10 00	1 15	4 30	10 05	4 30
2 42	8 17	12 52	7 17	7 10	6.5	......Starr......	9 41	12 52	4 12	9 48	4 12
2 47	8 22	12 57	7 21	7 16	8.5	......Mercer.....	9 35	12 46	4 08	9 43	4 08
2 51	8 26	12 41	7 25	7 25	10.0	....Newburn.....	9 30	12 41	4 05	9 39	4 05
3 00	8 35	12 50	7 35	7 37	14.0	....Lancaster...	9 18	12 19	3 54	9 29	3 54
3 10	8 45	1 05	7 45	8 20	17.0	..Dowling Park..	9 10	12 10	3 46	9 21	3 46
3 18	8 50	1 15	7 53	8 30	18.0	.....Chancey....	8 53	11 43	3 35	9 11	3 36
3 30	9 05	1 25	8 00	8 45	20.7	..Mayo Junction..	8 45	†11 35	3 30	9 05	3 30
3 36	9 10	1 35	8 05	A M	22.0	.....Day........	8 40	A M	3 25	9 00	3 25
3 43	9 17	1 47	8 12		25.0	.....Silo.......	8 26		3 17	8 52	3 17
3 51	9 23	1 59	8 21	▲	27.0	...Townsend.....	8 01	▲	3 11	8 46	3 11
4 04	9 36	2 19	8 36	27	33.0	.....Smith......	7 38	28	2 58	8 33	2 58
4 17	9 49	2 45	8 51	P M	38.0	...Fenholloway..	7 15	A M	2 45	8 20	2 45
4 35	10 05	3 30	9 15	ᵃ4 20	44.0	.....Perry².ᵟ	6 50	11 56	2 30	8 05	2 30
4 45	10 15	4 00	9 25	4 35	47.0	...Springdale...	6 20	11 37	2 16	7 51	2 17
4 52	10 23	4 10	9 32	4 39	48.0	...Pershing.....	6 03	11 27	2 08	7 43	2 10
4 55	10 26	4 15	9 36	4 42	49.0	Hampton Springs.	†6 00	11 24	2 05	§7 40	2 07
P M	10 50	P M	10 00	5 06	55.0	..Deavers' Mill..	A M	11 00	1 52	A M	1 42
	11 10		10 25	5 26	60.0	....Waylonzo.....		10 41	1 10		1 24
	11 47		11 09	5 58	68.0	...Mandalay.....		10 03	12 24		12 50
	12 15		11 35	6 25	74.0	...Flint Rock....		*9 35	†12 00		§12 25
P M		A M	P M		ARRIVE	LEAVE	A M	Noon			P M

* Daily; † daily, except Sunday; § Sunday only; a daily, but on Sunday runs 25 minutes later. ▲ Motor car. ᵟ Telegraph stations.

LIVE OAK AND ALTON

17	15	9	7	5	Mls	June, 1925.	8	6	10	16	18
PM	PM	PM	PM	AM		LEAVE	AM	PM	PM	AM	PM
§2 25	§8 00	†12 15	†12 15	†7 00	0	.....Live Oak¹..ᵟ	10 00	1 15	4 30	10 05	4 30
2 42	8 17	12 32	12 32	7 17	6.5	......Starr......	9 41	12 52	4 12	9 48	4 12
2 47	8 22	12 37	12 37	7 21	8.5	......Mercer.....	9 35	12 46	4 08	9 43	4 08
2 51	8 26	12 41	12 41	7 25	10.0	....Newburn.....	9 30	12 41	4 05	9 39	4 05
3 00	8 35	12 50	12 50	7 35	14.0	....Lancaster...	9 18	12 19	3 54	9 29	3 54
3 10	8 45	1 05	1 05	7 45	17.0	..Dowling Park.ᵟ	9 10	12 10	3 46	9 21	3 46
3 18	8 53	1 15	1 15	7 53	18.0	.....Chancey....	8 53	11 43	3 36	9 11	3 36
3 30	9 05	3 35	1 25	8 45	20.7	..Mayo Junction.	8 45	11 35	3 30	9 05	3 30
3 47	9 22	3 50	1 40	9 00	25.5	.......Dell......	7 33	11 20	3 08	8 33	3 03
3 58	9 33	4 01	1 51	9 12	29.0	.....Peterson...	7 22	11 08	2 57	8 22	2 52
4 09	9 44	4 13	2 02	9 40	32.7	......Mayo......	7 10	10 55	2 46	8 10	2 40
4 20	9 55	4 25	2 15	9 50	35.0	.....Alton....ᵟ	†7 00	†10 45	†2 35	§8 00	§2 50
P M		P M	A M	A M		ARRIVE	LEAVE A M	A M	P M	P M	P M

Connections.—¹ With Atlantic Coast Line R.R. and Seaboard Air Line Ry. ² With South Georgia Ry. and Atlantic Coast Line R.R.

Logs and lumber were the chief commodities hauled on the Live Oak, Perry & Gulf, but it also operated a clutch of passenger trains. Someday a book on Florida's amazing logging railroads will be written.

Even though the South Georgia Railway was based in Georgia, its main line descended into Florida to reach Perry and Hampton Springs, an area hardly affected by the boom.

SOUTH GEORGIA RAILWAY COMPANY.

J. W. Oglesby, President.
C. T. Tillman, Vice-President, Treasurer and Purchasing Agt.
R. C. McIntosh, Vice-President.
C. F. Cater, Secretary and Auditor.
C. H. Myers, Gen. Fht. and Pas. Agt.
J. W. Oglesby, Jr., Gen. Mgr.
W. M. Leverett, Superintendent.
J. J. Davis, Master Mechanic.
C. E. Clark, Trainmaster and Car Acct.
Branch & Snow, General Counsel.
General Offices—Quitman, Ga.

5	1	3	Mls.	December 15, 1925.	2	4	6
A M	P M	A M		LEAVE] [ARRIVE	A M	P M	P M
§7 30	*4 25	†7 30	0	.........Adel¹.........	11 45	7 10	7 30
7 54	4 50	8 00	10.8	.........Barney........	11 09	6 40	7 10
8 08	5 05	8 20	15.7	.........Morven........	10 57	6 25	7 00
8 40	5 35	8 50	27.5	arr....Quitman²...lve.	10 30	5 40	6 30
9 00	5 45	9 30	27.5	lve....Quitman....arr.	9 30	4 40	6 25
9 10	5 55	9 45	31.5	.......Rountree........	9 16	4 30	6 17
9 33	6 15	10 10	38.5	........Lovett........	9 00	4 05	5 55
9 51	6 30	10 35	45.8	........Dennett........	8 42	3 45	5 37
10 05	6 47	11 00	50.4	......Greenville³.....	8 30	3 30	5 25
10 26	7 05	11 35	59.0	........Sirmans........	8 08	3 00	5 00
10 35	7 13	11 50	63.8	......Shady Grove......	8 00	2 44	4 50
10 41	7 18	11 58	66.3	.......Lake Bird.......	7 55	2 37	4 45
10 54	7 28	12 20	70.7	.........Boyd.........	7 45	2 25	4 35
11 10	7 40	12 50	76.0	.........Perry⁴........	7 35	*2 00	4 20
11 50	8 00	P M	81.3	..Hampton Springs..	*7 15	P M	§4 00

Connections.—¹ With Ga. & Fla. Rys. ² With A. C. L. and Ga. So. & Fla. Rys. ³ With Se... ⁴ With Atlantic Coast Line and Live Oak, Perry & Gulf R. Rs.

Gulf R. Rs. — Atlantic Coast Line and Live Oak, Perry & Gulf R. Rs. Eastern time.

100

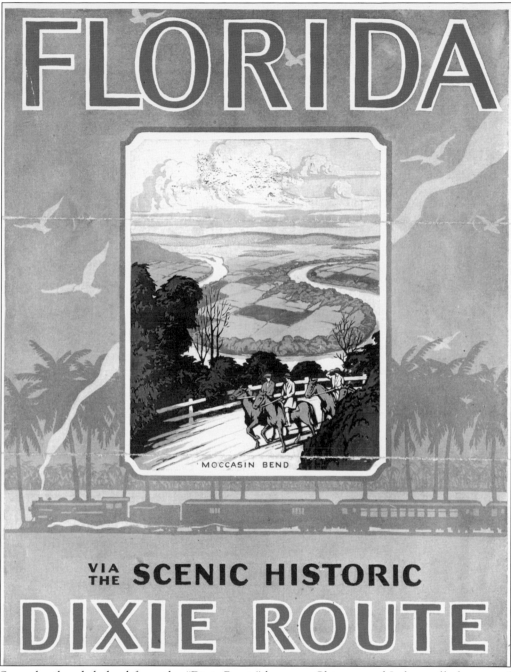

FLORIDA

MOCCASIN BEND

VIA THE SCENIC HISTORIC

DIXIE ROUTE

Several railroads helped form the "Dixie Route" between Chicago and Jacksonville by way of Nashville, Chattanooga, and Atlanta. The route traversed one of the most scenic and historic regions of the South, including the bluegrass farming region of Kentucky, along the Tennessee River, and around historic Lookout Mountain. From Chattanooga to Atlanta, it passed near Civil War battlefields and over the very course that Sherman followed on his famous march to the sea.

SCHEDULES

SOUTHBOUND READ DOWN				COMPLETE THROUGH SERVICE OF THE HISTORIC SCENIC DIXIE ROUTE	NORTHBOUND READ UP		
Dixie Limited	Dixie Express	Dixie Flyer All Pullman	Miles from Chicago		Dixie Flyer All Pullman	Dixie Express	Dixie Limited
Daily	Daily	Daily		Effective Southbound November 1st	Daily	Daily	
AM	PM	PM		*Via Chicago & Eastern Illinois Ry.*	AM	AM	PM
11.55	9.45	9.45	.0	Lv. Chicago (Dearborn Station)..(C.T.) Ar	7.45	7.45	4.10
......	9.55	9.55	4.6	Lv.....Forty-Seventh Street..... " Ar	7.32	7.32	3.57
12.10	10.00	10.00	6.6	Lv....Englewood (63d Street)..... " Ar	7.27	7.27	3.52
b	b	a	26.6	Lv....Chicago Heights ..... " Ar	e	h	h
b	b	a	49.9	Lv....Momence..... " Ar	e	h	h
b	b	a	77.5	Lv....Watseka..... " Ar	e	h	h
b	b	a	99.2	Lv....Hoopeston..... " Ar	e	h	h
2.57	12.52	12.52	123.2	Lv....Danville, Ill.... " Ar	4.01	4.01	12.45
4.25	2.27	2.27	177.5	Lv....Terre Haute, Ind.... " Ar	1.50	1.50	11.10
5.53	3.48	3.48	234.7	Lv....Vincennes, Ind.... " Ar	12.23	12.23	9.45
7.25	5.33	5.33	288.5	Ar Evansville, Ind. (L.&N. Station) " Lv	10.50	10.50	8.15
				Via Louisville & Nashville R. R.			
2.10	9.40	9.40	......	Lv........St. Louis, Mo........(C.T.) Ar	7.40	7.40	1.40
				Via Louisville & Nashville R. R.			
7.35	5.43	5.43	288.5	Lv........Evansville, Ind........(C.T.) Ar	10.40	10.40	8.05
12.10	10.17	10.17	447.2	Ar........Nashville, Tenn......... " Lv	5.40	5.40	3.20
				Via Nashville, Chattanooga & St. Louis Ry.			
12.17	10.27	10.27	447.2	Lv........Nashville, Tenn........(C.T.) Ar	5.25	5.25	3.13
......	11.18	......	478.0	Lv........Murfreesboro........ " Ar	† 4.30	4.30	......
4.15	2.37	2.37	598.9	Ar....Chattanooga, Tenn.... " Lv	1.00	1.00	11.10
4.25	2.47	2.47	598.9	Lv....Chattanooga, Tenn....... " Ar	12.51	12.51	11.00
......	3.43	......	636.7	Lv........Dalton, Ga.... " Ar	†11.45	11.45	......
8.00	6.29	6.29	735.7	Ar Atlanta, Ga. (Union Station). " Lv	9.00	9.00	7.20
				Via Central of Georgia Ry.			
8.20	7.45	6.50	735.7	Lv Atlanta, Ga.(Terminal Station)(C.T.) Ar	8.35	8.00	7.00
......	8.50	7.57	778.3	Lv........Griffin, Ga.... " Lv	7.17	6.43	......
11.00	10.20	9.35	838.4	Ar........Macon, Ga.... " Lv	5.45	5.10	4.10
11.05	10.25	9.40	838.4	Lv........Macon, Ga.... " Lv	5.40	5.00	4.05
1.06	12.20	11.42	908.9	Lv........Americus, Ga......... " Lv	3.20	2.53	2.06
2.05	1.25	12.42	944.6	Ar........Albany, Ga.... " Lv	2.25	1.55	1.10
				Via Atlantic Coast Line R. R.			
3.10	2.30	1.50	944.6	Lv........Albany, Ga........(E.T.) Ar	3.15	2.40	2.00
4.25	3.52	3.15	985.3	Ar........Tifton, Ga.... " Lv	1.48	1.24	12.40
6.35	5.50	5.10	1056.4	Ar........Waycross, Ga.... " Lv	11.50	11.15	10.35
8.40	8.00	7.15	1131.6	Ar........Jacksonville, Fla.... " Lv	9.45	9.10	8.30
				Via Florida East Coast Ry.			
9.50	....	(8)7.45	1131.6	Lv....Jacksonville, Fla........(E.T.) Ar	9.00	....	7.30
10.55	....	8.45	1168.6	Ar....St. Augustine, Fla.... " Lv	8.00	....	6.30
1.25	....	11.15	1241.6	Ar...Daytona Beach, Fla..... " Lv	5.30	....	4.00
8.00	....	5.55	1430.6	Ar...West Palm Beach, Fla...... " Lv	10.50	....	9.20
(5)10.35	....	8.30	1497.6	Ar....Miami, Fla.... " Lv	(7)8.15	....	(6)6.45
				Via Atlantic Coast Line R. R.			
(10)10.00	....	(9)9.00	1131.6	Lv....Jacksonville, Fla........(E.T.) Ar	7.00	....	(2)7.30
(1)8.15	....	5.00	1406.6	Ar....St. Petersburg, Fla.... " Lv	(9)11.15	....	(10)(2)9.00
				Via Atlantic Coast Line R. R.			
(3)10.00	....	8.00	1131.6	Lv....Jacksonville, Fla......... " Ar	7.35	....	(4)7.15
(3)7.00	....	3.00	1369.6	Ar...Tampa, Fla. (Via Orlando) " " Lv	12.15	....	(4)9.30
......	......	6.15	1410.6	Ar...Bradenton, Fla. " " " Lv	10.00	......	......
......	......	6.45	1422.6	Ar....Sarasota, Fla.. " " " Lv	9.35	......	......
AM	AM	PM			PM	PM	

Three separate Dixie Route trains were running to Florida in 1925: the *Dixie Flyer*, the *Dixie Express*, and the *Dixie Limited*. The Chicago & Eastern Illinois Railroad handled the trio between Chicago and Evansville, whereupon the Louisville & Nashville delivered each to Nashville proper. Then Dixie Route trains were handed over to the Nashville, Chattanooga & St. Louis Railway

EQUIPMENT

Dixie Flyer All-Pullman *through* to Miami

CLUB LOUNGE CAR (Maid and Valet Service) . . . . Between Chicago and Miami.

OBSERVATION SLEEPING CAR (Open Section) . . . . Between Chicago and Miami.

COMPARTMENT DRAWING-ROOM SLEEPING CARS . . . . . . Between Chicago and Miami.
Between Chicago and Jacksonville.

DRAWING-ROOM AND OPEN-SECTION SLEEPING CARS . Between Chicago and Miami.
Between Chicago and St. Petersburg.
Between Chicago, Tampa and Sarasota.
Between Chicago and Jacksonville.
Between St. Louis and Miami.
Between St. Louis, Tampa and Sarasota.
Between St. Louis and Jacksonville.

DINING CAR . . . . For all meals.

NOTE: Dixie Flyer southbound carries passengers to points south of Atlanta only;
northbound carries passengers from Chattanooga and south only.

Dixie Express

OBSERVATION SLEEPING CAR (Open Sections) . . . . Between Chicago and Atlanta—Jacksonville.

DRAWING-ROOM AND OPEN-SECTION SLEEPING CAR . . Between Chicago and Jacksonville.
Between Chicago and Atlanta—Jacksonville.
Between Evansville and Jacksonville
(ready for occupancy at Evansville at 9.00 p.m.).
Between St. Louis and Jacksonville.

COACHES . . . . Between Chicago and Jacksonville.
Between St. Louis and Jacksonville with
one change of cars en route.

DINING CAR . . . . For all meals.

Dixie Limited

OBSERVATION SLEEPING CAR (Open Sections) . . . . Between Chicago and Jacksonville.

COMPARTMENT AND DRAWING-ROOM SLEEPING CARS . . Between Chicago and Miami.
Between Chicago and Palm Beach.
Between Chicago and Jacksonville.

DRAWING-ROOM, OPEN-SECTION SLEEPING CARS . . . . Between Chicago and St. Petersburg.
Between Chicago and Tampa.
Between Chicago and Jacksonville.
Between Chicago and Miami.

for the journey to Atlanta. At Atlanta, the Central of Georgia played host to Albany, where the famous consists were handed off to the Atlantic Coast Line Railroad for Jacksonville. Service between "Jax" and Miami was handled by the Florida East Coast Railway, while the ACL offered connecting service to such destinations as Tampa, Sarasota, and St. Petersburg.

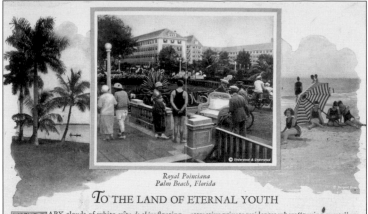

Royal Poinciana
Palm Beach, Florida

To THE LAND OF ETERNAL YOUTH

ABY clouds of white *crêpe de chine* floating against a sapphire sky. A friendly sun urging you to come out in it for a coat of youthful tan. Tall, stately palms beckoning indolently to you. Long silver strands of firm, white beach caressed by a lazy coaxing surf that bids you to a refreshing dip in it. Bewitching streams and lagoons arched by great, old, moss-draped trees glamoured by an urgent tropic moon. Golden days full of the lyric quality of gay young voices. Enchanted nights charmed with the magic of dreamy music floating over lake and lagoon from portico and patio.

This is Florida—intriguing, amorous Florida. Land of Eternal Youth. Blessed with the most equable climate in all the world; a coast line longer than any state in the Union; year-round swimming and boating; an incomparable vacation land. Fishing enough to satiate the most ardent angler—every variety of deep-sea and fresh-water fish. Golf courses that, at sight of them, make your hands tingle for a driver. Perfect tennis courts. Palatial hotels with nationally famous dance orchestras. Comfortable American-plan hotels, only a trifle less luxurious, for the less affluent. Picturesque little bungalow colonies. Modest but always

attractive private residences where "paying guests" are made to feel "at home." And flowers—flowers— everywhere. The tang and fragrance of growing things. Vine-covered pergolas, waving palms, flaming poinsettias. Color! Play! Life! Florida!

A DIXIE ROUTE train is waiting for you, waiting to transport you in luxury to the golden land of heart's desire through a country flooded with color, a country full to the brim with memories of the epic days of '61.

If you go DIXIE ROUTE you don't set out just to get there. It's the route the accustomed Florida traveler prefers. And, like as not, you'll meet a lot of the "old timers" aboard who have traveled the DIXIE ROUTE all their lives; and there'll be a lot of familiar faces among the younger set who most naturally prefer the colorful route to colorful Florida."

You'll re-live other seasons and make lots of plans for this one. When you arrive at your destination there'll be mingled with your pleasurable anticipations about Florida a queer little regret that the journey's over and a whole lot of satisfaction about the meals, the service, the comforts, and the scenery of the DIXIE ROUTE—"Mile for mile America's most interesting trip."

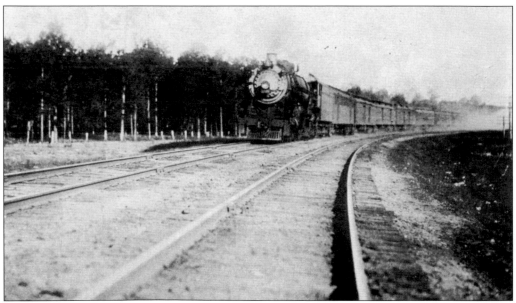

In this 1926 view, the *Dixie Express* rounds the long curve at Moncrief near Jacksonville. (Courtesy Railway and Locomotive Historical Society.)

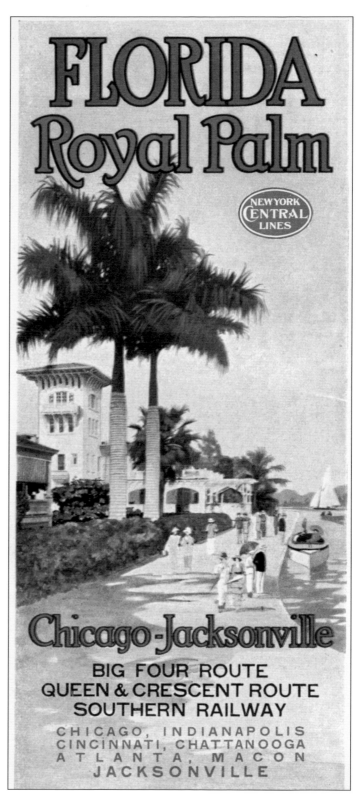

FLORIDA
Royal Palm

NEW YORK
CENTRAL
LINES

Chicago-Jacksonville

BIG FOUR ROUTE
QUEEN & CRESCENT ROUTE
SOUTHERN RAILWAY

CHICAGO, INDIANAPOLIS
CINCINNATI, CHATTANOOGA
ATLANTA, MACON
JACKSONVILLE

Another prestigious, boom-era train that served Florida from Chicago was the *Royal Palm.* As this 1926 timetable notes, it was jointly operated by several railroads. Alluring scenes adorned each timetable cover, and often they motivated tourists into action.

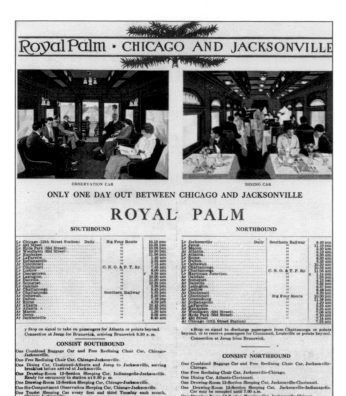

This *Royal Palm* booklet described the train from soup to nuts, including a recitation of every station stop.

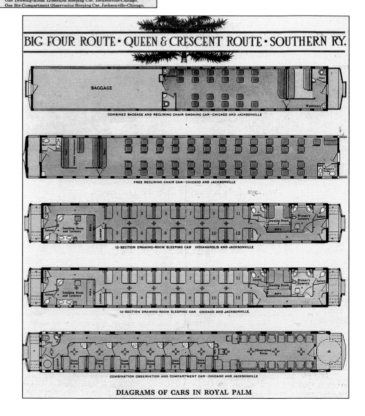

The aforementioned booklet also contained drawings of each car interior.

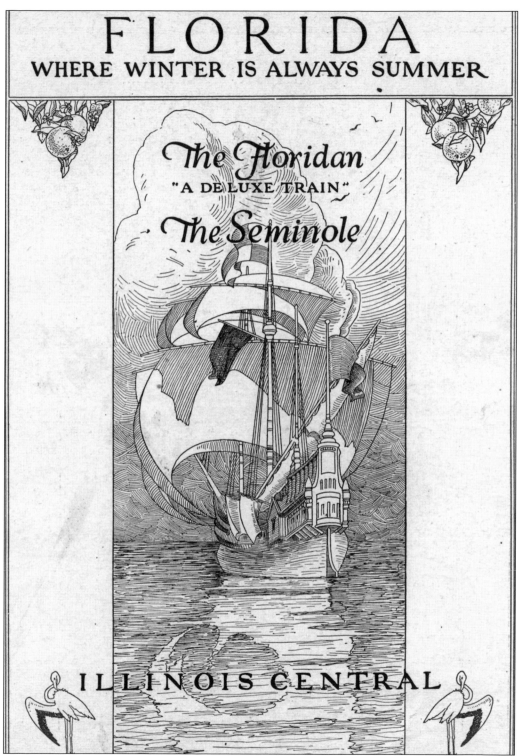

FLORIDA
WHERE WINTER IS ALWAYS SUMMER

The Floridan
"A DE LUXE TRAIN"

The Seminole

ILLINOIS CENTRAL

Many tourists from the Midwest went to Florida on trains operated by the Illinois Central Railroad. Two famous IC trains were *The Floridan* and *The Seminole*.

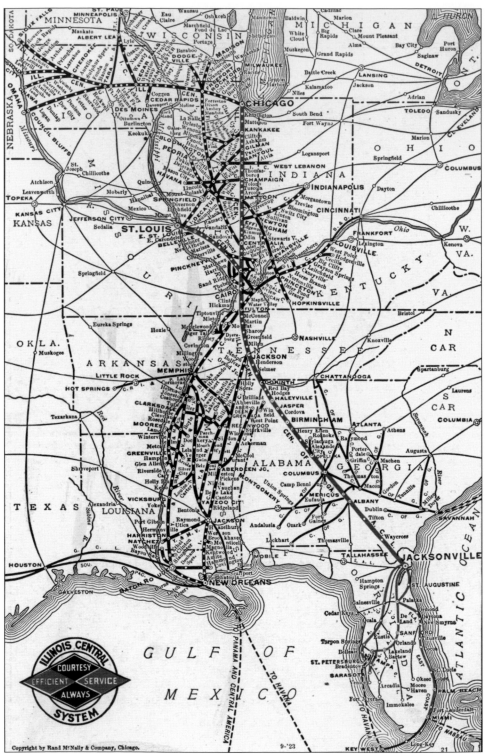

A system map of the Illinois Central shows how its trains reached Florida, in conjunction with other carriers.

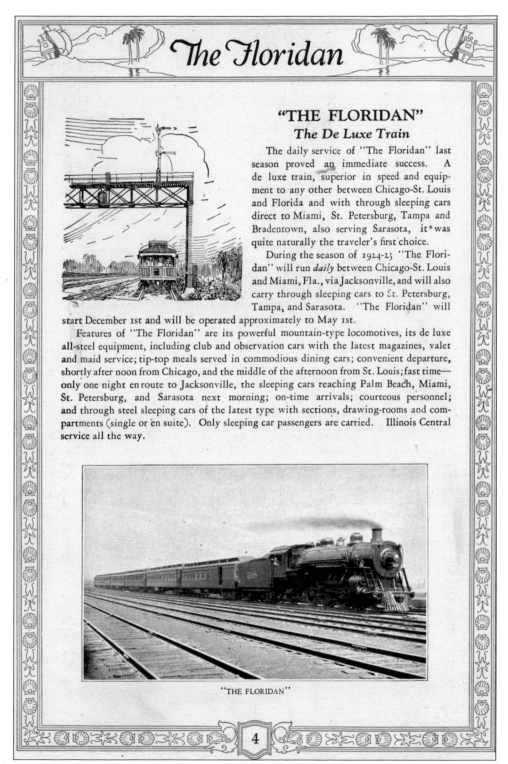

The Floridan

"THE FLORIDAN"
The De Luxe Train

The daily service of "The Floridan" last season proved an immediate success. A de luxe train, superior in speed and equipment to any other between Chicago-St. Louis and Florida and with through sleeping cars direct to Miami, St. Petersburg, Tampa and Bradentown, also serving Sarasota, it was quite naturally the traveler's first choice.

During the season of 1924-25 "The Floridan" will run *daily* between Chicago-St. Louis and Miami, Fla., via Jacksonville, and will also carry through sleeping cars to St. Petersburg, Tampa, and Sarasota. "The Floridan" will start December 1st and will be operated approximately to May 1st.

Features of "The Floridan" are its powerful mountain-type locomotives, its de luxe all-steel equipment, including club and observation cars with the latest magazines, valet and maid service; tip-top meals served in commodious dining cars; convenient departure, shortly after noon from Chicago, and the middle of the afternoon from St. Louis; fast time— only one night en route to Jacksonville, the sleeping cars reaching Palm Beach, Miami, St. Petersburg, and Sarasota next morning; on-time arrivals; courteous personnel; and through steel sleeping cars of the latest type with sections, drawing-rooms and compartments (single or en suite). Only sleeping car passengers are carried. Illinois Central service all the way.

"THE FLORIDAN"

4

A large clientele patronized *The Floridan*, which ran on a daily basis in the 1924 winter season. Only sleeping car customers were transported.

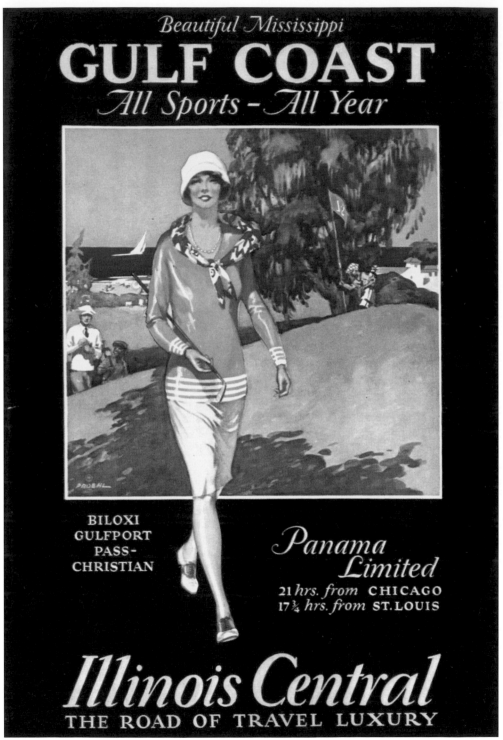

The Illinois Central Railroad owned no tracks in Florida. However, in the May 1925 issue of *Nation's Business* magazine, it was reported that the company was buying a right-of-way into the Sunshine State and down the Gulf coast. Proof of the rumor is still lacking.

Six

WHY THEY CAME

So far this book has focused on railroad companies, events, and statistics. But what about the people who came to Florida during the 1920s? Why did they come? What did they do once they got here? In the pages that remain, we explore these very questions.

Naturally many folks descended upon the Sunshine State as newcomers or to invest in or sell real estate. Once the boom got underway, Northern newspapers and magazines published favorable articles about the land and growing real estate fever. This helped bring the crowds to Florida by car, boat, and bus, but literally millions came that decade by train.

Florida's railroads also chased another important market: tourists and vacationers, persons who were not interested in buying or selling anything. They just wanted a winter vacation, a place to unwind. Many of these customers were or became infatuated with the state's countless beaches. Others came to boat, fish, golf, be pampered at hotels, or to visit the top tourist attractions. And all this could be done without fear of harsh weather. When blizzards eventually gripped the North, the railroads were quick to flash this simple message: IT'S JUNE IN MIAMI.

Yes, Florida was indeed a magical place for travelers, and it remains so today. Getting to the "land of eternal youth" was fun in the 1920s, especially aboard a crack passenger train. You slept soundly in a clean Pullman berth, meals in the dining car were an event, and America unfolded at one's window.

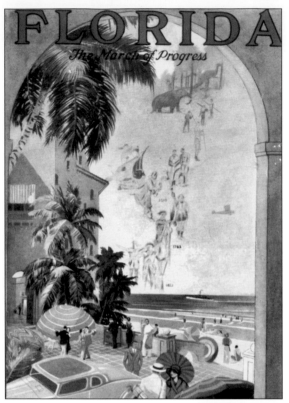

Colorful booklets about Florida appeared before the First World War. This one surfaced in 1922, just as the land boom was getting underway.

Florida's railroads always wanted winter-weary tourists. The quest never stopped. This booklet was prepared by the Florida East Coast Railway.

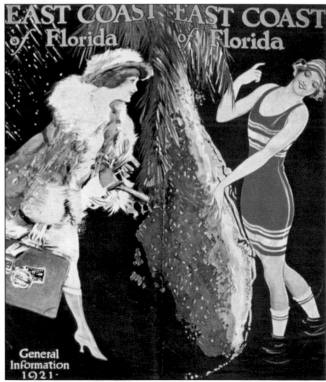

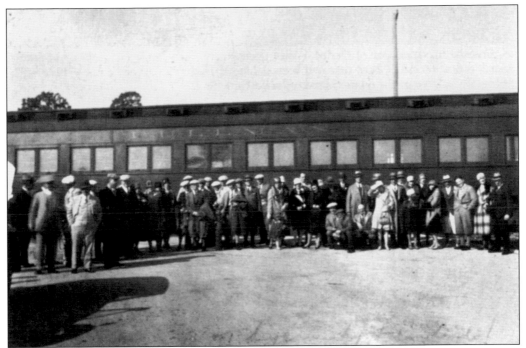

Naturally countless people came to Florida in the 1920s to buy or sell real estate. This Pullman load of prospects has just arrived at Dunedin from Michigan. (Courtesy Florida State Photo Archives.)

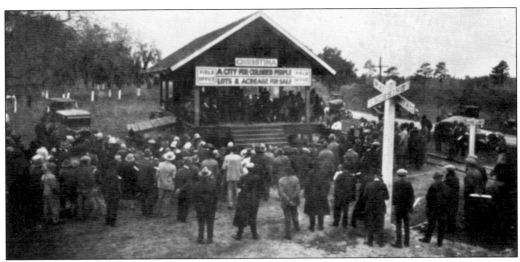

At Christina, near Winston, a "City for Colored People" was advertised. Prospects came by train, and building lots sold like hotcakes. (Courtesy Florida State Photo Archives.)

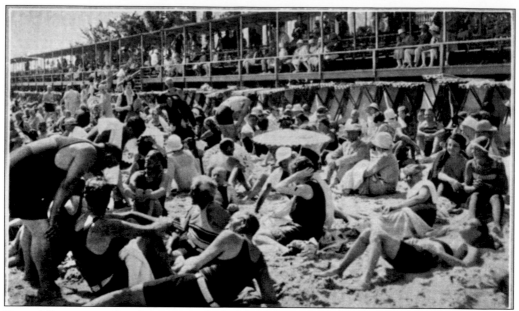

Some folks came to Florida just to go the beach. This 1925 image was snapped near New Smyrna.

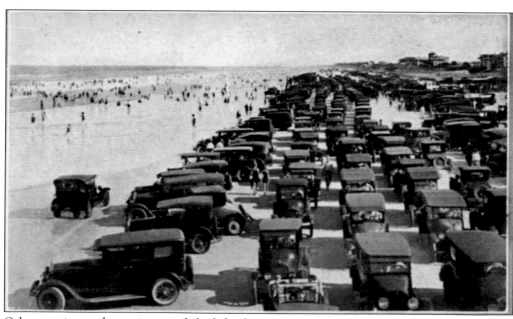

Other tourists and vacationers relished the fun at Daytona Beach, where cars could be driven on the packed sand.

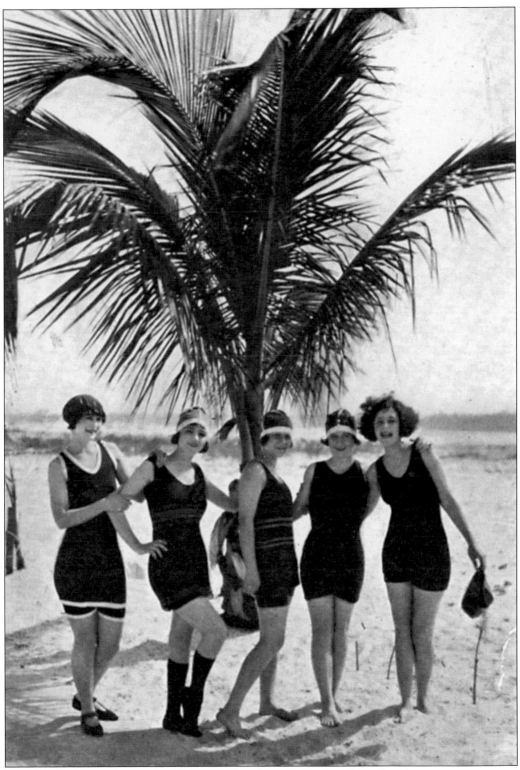

Standing under a palm tree at Clearwater Beach was sure nicer than shoveling snow.

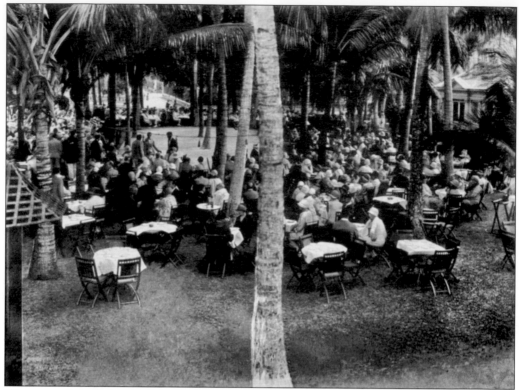

The upper class often sipped drinks in the Cocoanut Grove at Palm Beach. Dressing in Bermuda shorts and knit shirts was definitely taboo.

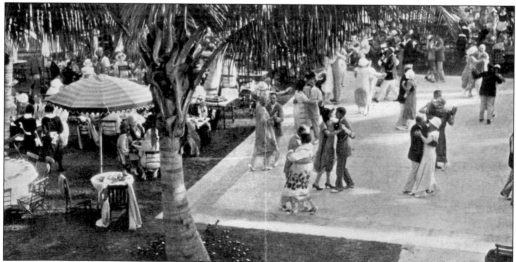

Some hotel guests danced after lunch. Why not?

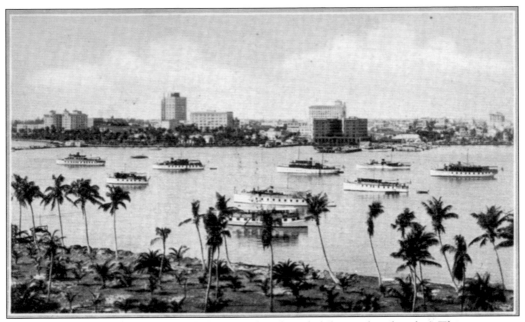

The well-to-do often came to Florida by train then boarded their palatial yachts. This scene was snapped at Palm Beach.

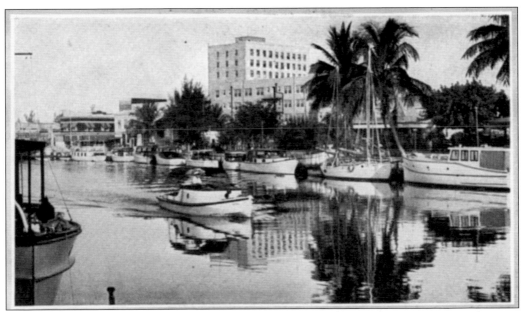

The not-so-wealthy had just as much fun on their pleasure craft, like these boaters on the New River in Fort Lauderdale.

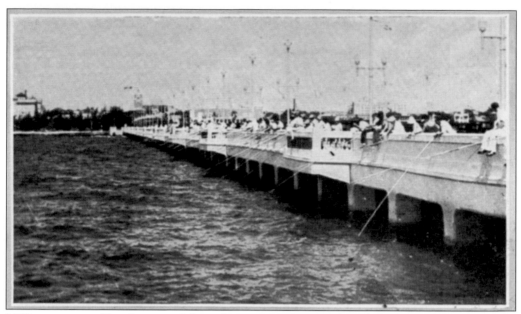

Millions came to Florida just to fish, as this scene at St. Petersburg helps confirm.

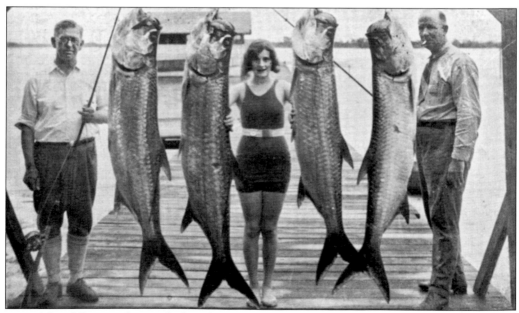

Some fisher folk wanted to catch the Silver King—tarpon. This trio in Fort Myers hit the jackpot.

118

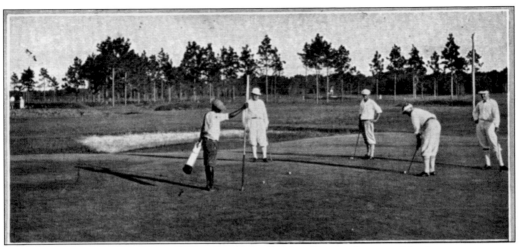

Golf has always been great fun in Florida. After all, it's a 12-month proposition!

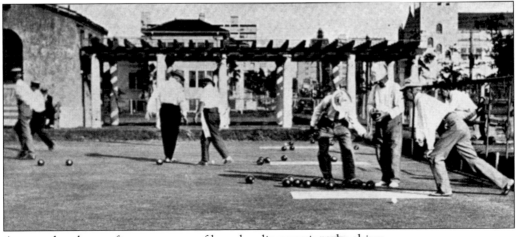

At many hotels, an afternoon game of lawn bowling was just the thing.

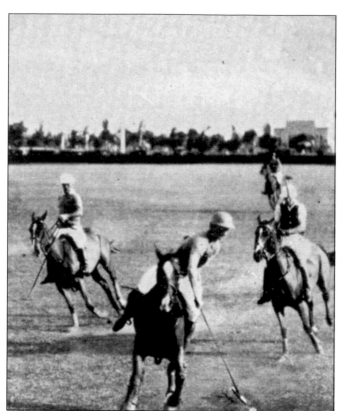

At the Miami Polo Club, the action was non-stop.

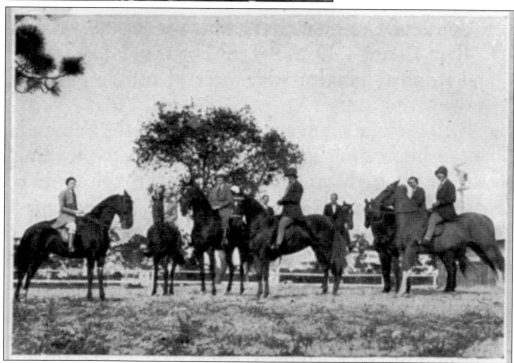

Horseback riding was a great way to see the countryside, especially near Ocala.

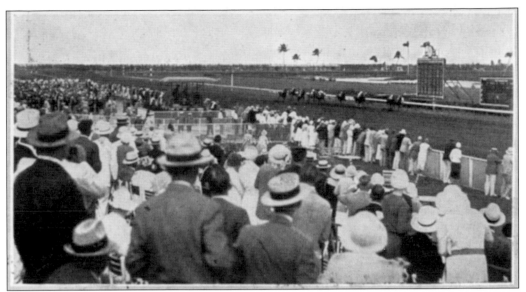

Florida had many beautiful racetracks. This one was operated by the Miami Jockey Club.

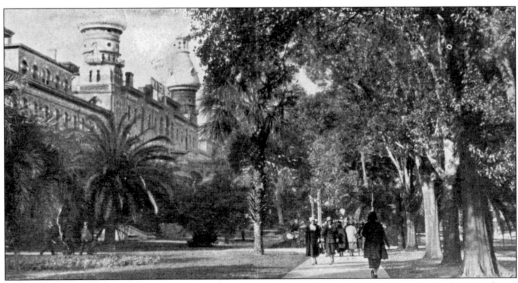

Just a walk in the Florida sun could warm those Northern bones. This image was taken in front of the Tampa Bay Hotel.

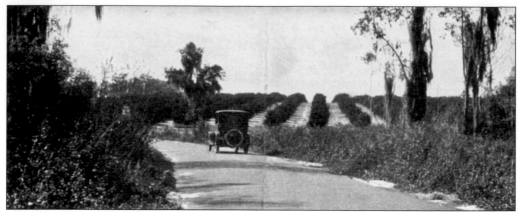

Some winter visitors had to get behind a wheel. This motorcar is meandering past orange groves near Lake Wales. No wonder the region was called the "Scenic Highlands."

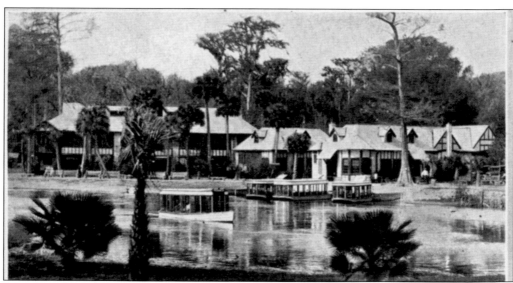

Florida was loaded with tourist attractions. A popular destination was Silver Springs with its glass-bottom boats.

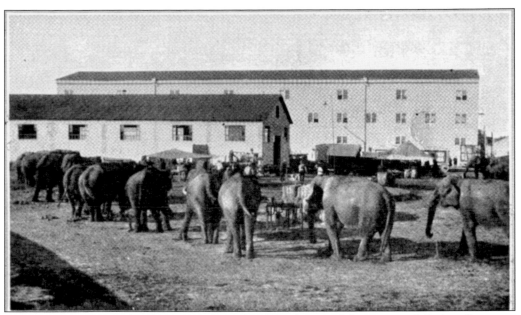

A visit to the winter headquarters of Ringling Brothers and Barnum and Bailey Circus in Sarasota was always a treat.

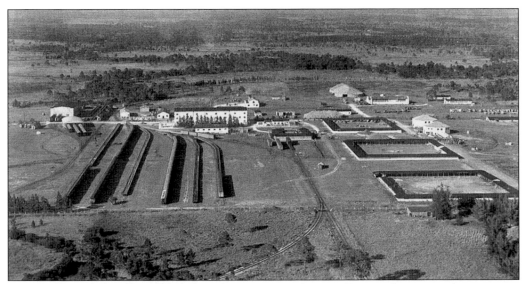

The Ringling circus moved about the country in special trains. During the winter, the cars were parked in their Sarasota rail yard, visible at left.

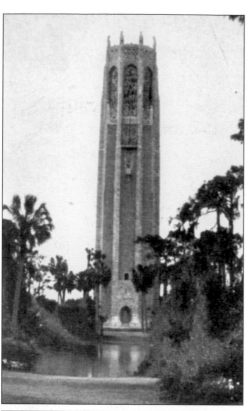

Then as now, a top state attraction was the Bok Tower carillon in Lake Wales. To miss it was unforgivable.

And how did the carillon bells get to Lake Wales?

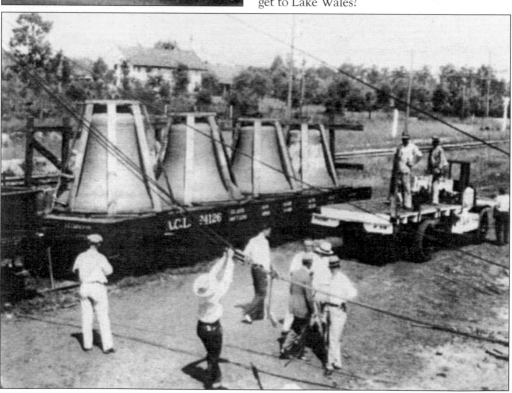

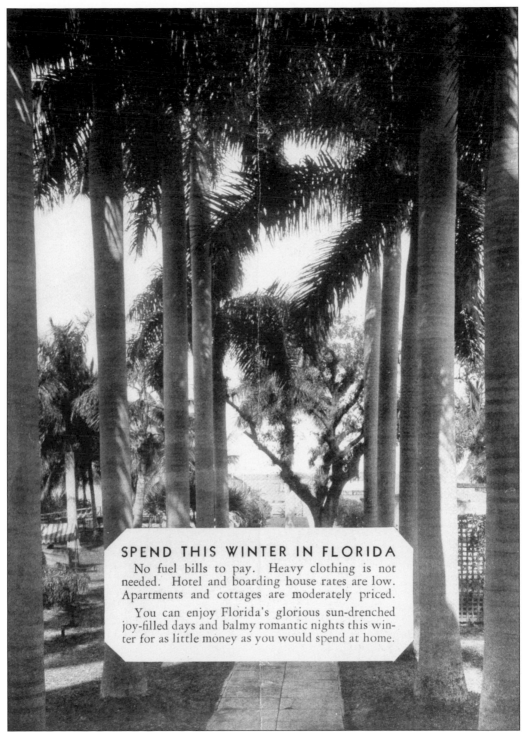

SPEND THIS WINTER IN FLORIDA

No fuel bills to pay. Heavy clothing is not needed. Hotel and boarding house rates are low. Apartments and cottages are moderately priced.

You can enjoy Florida's glorious sun-drenched joy-filled days and balmy romantic nights this winter for as little money as you would spend at home.

This inviting advertisement was prepared in the 1920s by the Atlantic Coast Line Railroad.

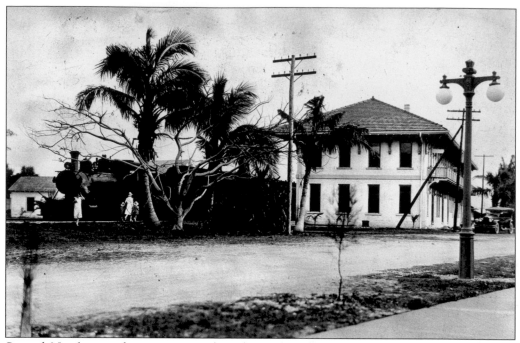

Several Northerners have just arrived at the Seaboard's Boca Grande station. Their island chariot waits at the far right.

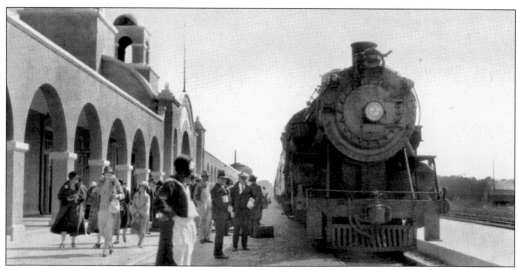

The Orlando station of the Atlantic Coast Line Railroad always seemed busy. Time to shed those heavy winter coats!

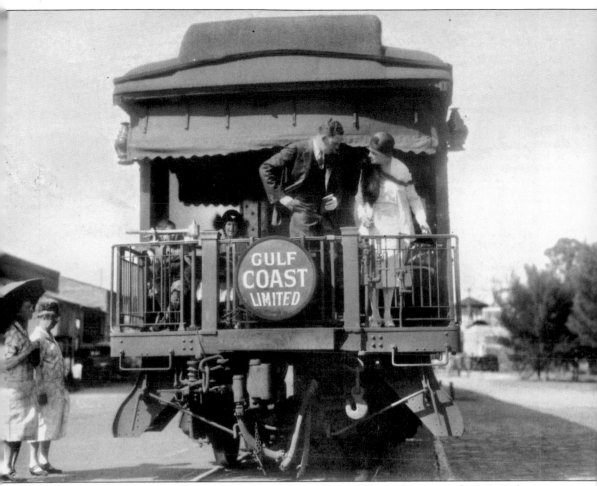

The Atlantic Coast Line Railroad inaugurated the *Gulf Coast Limited* in December 1927 along with the *Miamian*. The former ran between New York and the central and west coast regions of Florida. Here it is about to depart sunny St. Petersburg one year later. Seats on the parlor car's observation deck are starting to fill up.

FURTHER READING

Allen, Frederick Lewis. *Only Yesterday, An Informal History of the 1920s*. New York: Harper and Row Publishers, 1931.

Bramson, Seth. *Speedway to Sunshine*. Erin, Ontario: The Boston Mills Press, 2003.

Campbell, Walter E. *Across Fortune's Tracks, A Biography of William Rand Kenan, Jr.* Chapel Hill, NC: The University of North Carolina Press, 1996.

Florida Theme Issue. The Journal of Decorative and Propaganda Arts. Miami: Wolfsonian-Florida International University, 1998.

Hoffman, Glenn. *A History of the Atlantic Coast Line Railroad Company*. Jacksonville, FL: CSX Corporation, 1998.

Key, R. Lyle Jr. *Midwest Florida Sunliners*. Godfrey, IL: RPC Publications, 1979.

Nolan, David. *Fifty Feet in Paradise, The Booming of Florida*. New York: Harcourt, Brace and Jovanovich Publishers, 1884.

Railway Age Magazine articles: *Florida Travel Illustrates Increase in Passenger Service* (March 31, 1928); *Florida Roads Have Experienced a Phenomenal Development* (November 19, 1927); *Florida Roads Spent Millions in Construction During Boom* (November 26, 1927); *Permit Plan to Aid Florida Rail Congestion* (January 23, 1926); *Enormous Increase in Florida Traffic* (November 28, 1925).

Shrady, Theodore and Arthur M. Waldrop. *Orange Blossom Special, The Story of Florida's Distinguished Winter Train*. Valrico, FL: Atlantic Coast Line and Seaboard Air Line Railroad Historical Society, 2000.

Turner, Gregg M. *A Short History of Florida Railroads*. Charleston, SC: Arcadia Publishing, 2003.

———. *Railroads of Southwest Florida*. Charleston, SC: Arcadia Publishing, 1999.

———. *Venice in the 1920s*. Charleston, SC: Arcadia Publishing, 2000.

———. *A Milestone Celebration: The Seaboard Railway to Naples and Miami*. Bloomington, IN: Author House Publishing, 2004.